THE STORY OF EXPLORATION

EXPLORING
MOUNTAINS

ABDO
Publishing Company

THE STORY OF EXPLORATION

EXPLORING MOUNTAINS

BY LAURA PERDEW

CONTENT CONSULTANT
MAURICE ISSERMAN
PROFESSOR OF HISTORY
HAMILTON COLLEGE

CREDITS

Published by ABDO Publishing Company, PO Box 398166, Minneapolis, MN 55439. Copyright © 2014 by Abdo Consulting Group, Inc. International copyrights reserved in all countries. No part of this book may be reproduced in any form without written permission from the publisher. The Essential Library™ is a trademark and logo of ABDO Publishing Company.

Printed in the United States of America,
North Mankato, Minnesota
102013
012014

Editor: Rebecca Felix
Series Designer: Emily Love

Photo credits: iStockphoto/Thinkstock, cover, 1, 70–71, 99, 124–125, 128; Shutterstock Images, 6–7, 30; AP Images, 9, 133 (top right); Press Association/AP Images, 11; Galyna Andrushko/Shutterstock Images, 14–15, 133 (bottom right); Red Line Editorial, 17 (top), 17 (middle), 80–81, 132; Michael Studinger/NASA, 17 (bottom); Top Photo Group/Thinkstock, 18–19; Pictore/iStockphoto, 22; Photos.com/Getty Images/Thinkstock, 26–27, 32–33; Antonio Abrignani/Shutterstock Images, 28–29; Christian Kober/Robert Harding World Imagery/Corbis, 38; Bettmann/Corbis, 42, 89; Corbis, 47, 55; Hulton-Deutsch Collection/Corbis, 50–51; Mary Evans Picture Library/Alamy, 56; North Wind/North Wind Picture Archives, 60; Krzysztof Wiktor/Shutterstock Images, 62–63; Library of Congress, 65; Jonathan Griffith/Aurora Photos/Corbis, 66–67; My Good Images/Shutterstock Images, 74–75; Public Domain, 76, 133 (top left); Vittorio Sella/National Geographic Society/Corbis, 78–79; Design Pics/Thinkstock, 84–85; Imagno/Getty Images, 90–91; Jonathan Griffith/Aurora Photos/Corbis, 93; Comstock/Jupiterimages/Getty Images/Thinkstock, 95, 133 (bottom left); Jerry Cooke/Pix Inc./Time Life Pictures/Getty Images, 96; Daniel Prudek/Shutterstock Images, 102–103; STR/AP Images, 109; Keystone-France/Gamma-Keystone via Getty Images, 110; Pictorial Parade/Getty Images, 115; Vitalii Nesterchuk/Shutterstock Images, 116–117; Keystone/Hulton Archive/Getty Images, 120–121; SPCC/Xinhua Press/Corbis, 123

Library of Congress Control Number: 2013946599
Cataloging-in-Publication Data

Perdew, Laura.
 Exploring mountains / Laura Perdew.
   p. cm. -- (The story of exploration)
Includes bibliographical references and index.
ISBN 978-1-62403-251-6
1. Mountains--Juvenile literature. 2. Mountain ecology--Juvenile literature. 3. Mountains--Discovery and exploration--Juvenile literature. I. Title.
551.43--dc23

2013946599

CONTENTS

Mount Everest towers hundreds of feet higher above sea level than any other mountain in the world.

CHAPTER 1

MOUNTAIN EXPLORATION

Early on the morning of May 29, 1953, Tenzing Norgay and Edmund Hillary woke up in a tent. They were perched on the side of a mountain at 27,639 feet (8,424 m) above sea level, deep in the Himalayas. More than 16,000 feet (5,000 m) below them, Tenzing could see the smoke rising from Thyangboche monastery. Both men knew the monks would be making offerings for the climbers' safety. Above the climbers was the summit of Mount Everest, the world's highest mountain at 29,035 feet (8,850 m).[1]

Tenzing and Hillary had camped higher than anyone ever had before. They were poised to become the first to reach Everest's highest summit. Inside their small tent, Hillary lit the stove in order to thaw out his boots. Tenzing had worn his boots inside his sleeping bag all night. The pair also melted ice for water in order to prevent dehydration. At 6:30 a.m., Tenzing and Hillary emerged into the sunlight and began their ascent.

Roped together, Tenzing and Hillary kicked steps into the snow and ice of the steep southeast ridge. By 9:00 a.m. they had reached the lower, south summit. Then, with Hillary leading, they inched across a knifelike ridge. To one side was a 10,000-foot (3,050 m) drop. After crossing the ridge, the climbers came to a rocky cliff that was more than 65 feet (20 m) high. Hillary jammed his body in a crack and slowly wriggled his way up the cliff. Tenzing followed. At last the pair made it up the final, gently sloping ridge.

Edmund Hillary, *left*, and Tenzing Norgay, *right*, wearing the gear they used while becoming the first persons to reach the world's highest point

At 11:30 a.m., Tenzing and Hillary reached the highest point on Earth. Atop the mountain, Tenzing flung his arms around Hillary. "Tuji Chey, Chomolungma," he whispered.[2] This meant "thank you, Everest," as Chomolungma, which means "the goddess mountain," is the Tibetan Buddhist name for Everest.[3] Hillary left a crucifix from their expedition leader in the snow atop the summit. Tenzing's offerings included a pencil from his daughter and sweets.

MEASURING MOUNTAIN HEIGHT

A mountain's height is typically measured from sea level to summit. Measuring this way makes Everest in Asia the tallest mountain on Earth at 29,035 feet (8,850 m). However, surrounding the Hawaiian Islands is very deep ocean. The volcanic mountain Mauna Kea on the main island of Hawaii rises to 13,792 feet (4,205 m) above sea level. The greater, unseen part of the mountain, though, is under water. From the base of the mountain to sea level, the mountain rises 19,700 feet (6,000 m). Add the numbers together and Mauna Kea is actually 33,492 feet (10,205 m) tall. Thus, if measured from base to peak, Mauna Kea is the tallest mountain on Earth.[4]

MOUNTAIN EXPLORATION

After Tenzing and Hillary succeeded, other expedition teams plotted the first ascent of the 13 other 8,000-meter (26,247 ft) peaks in the Himalayan region of Asia. One century earlier, explorers had similarly scrambled to make the first ascent of the

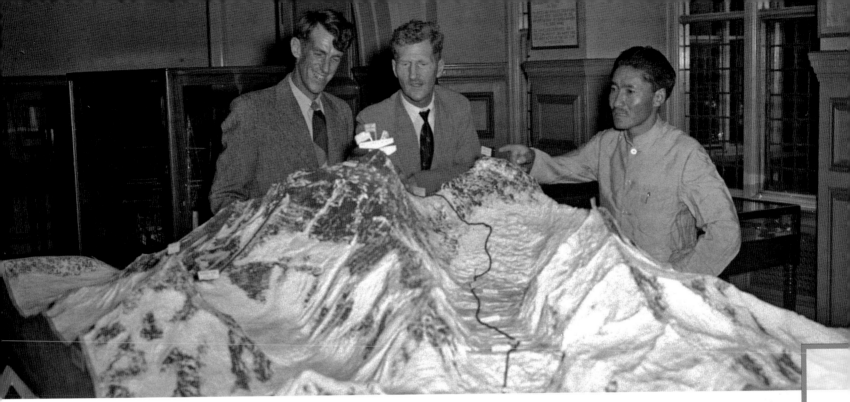

Standing beside expedition leader John Hunt (*center*), Hillary, and Tenzing describe their summit of Everest, which earned them much praise and inspired other climbers to plan similar summit bids.

tallest peaks in the European Alps. Yet in the span of human history, the notion that mountains were places to be explored or summited for personal satisfaction is relatively new. With only a few exceptions, people did not regularly travel into the mountains for exploration until the mid-1800s.

SEVEN SUMMITS

In Asia, the Himalayas hold the highest mountain in the world, Everest, at 29,035 feet (8,850 m). The Caucasus Mountains in eastern Europe contain that continent's tallest mountain, 18,510-foot- (5,642 m) tall Mount Elbrus.[5] Mount Kilimanjaro is Africa's highest peak at 19,340 feet (5,895 m).[6] In Australia, the Great Dividing Range runs along the east coast. Within the range, in the Snowy Mountains, is Mount Kosciuszko, the highest summit in Australia at 7,310 feet (2,228 m).[7] Antarctica's tallest is Vinson Massif, which lies in the Ellsworth Mountains and reaches 16,050 feet (4,892 m).[8]

The grandest range in South America is the Andes, which is the longest system in the world, extending 5,500 miles (8,851 km)—nearly the length of the entire continent.[9] Within the Andes is the highest peak in South America, 22,841-foot (6,962 m) Aconcagua.[10] In North America lies the Alaska Range, where Mount McKinley, also called Denali, the continent's tallest peak, extends 20,320 feet (6,194 m) high.[11]

Instead, mountains were traversed out of necessity when migrating or traveling on trade routes or for religious purposes. No matter the reason, the first to venture onto mountains did so with uncertainty and even fear. Little was understood about mountains. They were essentially unexplored and unmapped. Every step was one into the unknown.

There are mountains on each of the world's seven continents. Taken together, the highest peak on each of the continents are today known by climbers as the Seven Summits. Ranges in each corner of the world have been explored since the beginning of mountain exploration. But attitudes toward mountain exploration today differ greatly from early history. Mountains inspired myth and were shrouded in mystery throughout much of history. Mountain climbers face dangers such as avalanches, storms, hypothermia, exhaustion, and lack of oxygen at high elevations. Even today, plummeting thousands of feet down a rocky mountainside is an ever-present threat. Climbers take on great challenge, but in exchange they witness amazing sights and discoveries. Mountains contain great beauty and amazing scientific and historical discoveries, including mummies, archaeological artifacts, hidden caves, and rich ecosystems. They are mystical, towering places of snow and ice, jagged rock, and

MOUNTAIN ECOSYSTEMS

Mountains have a variety of ecosystems. The forest zone is at the base of most mountains. Depending on location, there are deciduous and coniferous trees, and in other places tropical vegetation. At tree line, the forest gives way to low lying shrubs and smaller flora such as grasses, thickets, herbs, and wildflowers. These perennial alpine plants are well adapted to the altitude and short growing season.

With further altitude gains, the plants thin out. The landscape at these altitudes is dominated by rock fields, boulders, scree, and barren soil. This is where the weather is too severe for any type of plant to survive. On the world's highest mountains, at the highest zones, are snow and ice. At this snowline, the snow, glaciers, and ice are permanent. The average temperature does not exceed 32 degrees Fahrenheit (0°C).

The challenge, beauty, and mystery of the mountains inspires exploration around the world.

dizzying heights. Mountain summits reach into the clouds, inspiring awe and begging exploration, challenging explorers to take them on. As climber Albert Mummery explained,

> *The true mountaineer is a wanderer . . . a man who loves to be where no human being has been before, who delights in gripping rocks that have previously never felt the touch of human fingers. . . . Equally, whether he succeeds or fails, he delights in the fun and jollity of the struggle.*[12]

EXPEDITION IN FOCUS
VINSON MASSIF, ANTARCTICA (1966)

By 1966, six of the Seven Summits had been climbed. Yet the highest peak on the Antarctic continent lay untouched. While not the highest of the seven, Vinson Massif, which is also often called Mount Vinson and rises 16,050 feet (4,892 m), is the most remote. The peak is in the Ellsworth Mountains, on a desertlike continent of ice that includes the South Pole. It has no permanent population, indigenous people, or government. Temperatures there reach minus 90 degrees Fahrenheit (-68°C), with temperatures in the warmest months ranging up to five degrees Fahrenheit (-15°C).[13]

In 1963, two different groups lobbied for funds to support an expedition to Antarctica. Ultimately they joined forces. The American Antarctic Mountaineering Expedition 1966/67 was sponsored by various organizations, including the National Geographic Society. The all-American team of ten was supported by the US Navy and the National Science Foundation. The group traveled from New Zealand to a US Navy base at McMurdo Sound. From there they flew further inland on a transport

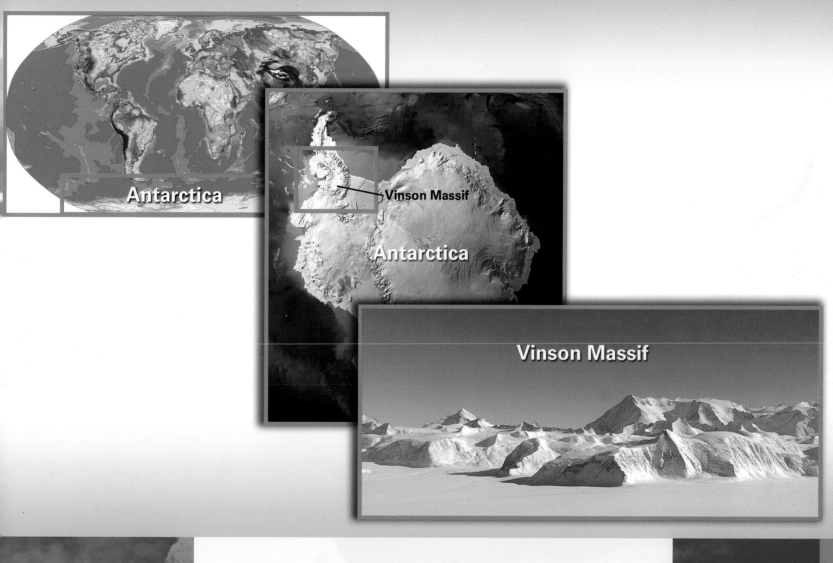

Antarctica

Antarctica

Vinson Massif

Vinson Massif

aircraft fitted with skis. On December 17, 1966, the first of the team reached the summit. The others followed within the next two days.

It is believed the site of ancient Incan city Machu Picchu was chosen for religious purposes, a main inspiration for mountain exploration across the world for centuries.

CHAPTER 2

EARLY CLIMBERS

In early history, most people were wary of mountains. Early cultures regarded mountains with a general feeling of fear or divine respect. In many early religions, mountains were heralded as the setting for divine activities and residence. People traveled to sacred mountains to worship. In ancient Greece, people believed gods lived on Mount Olympus, where they watched over mortals. Some believed mountains were home to angry dragons that were dangerous when provoked.

Mountain exploration evokes a variety of feelings around the world. Even as greater numbers of scientists trekked into the mountains in search of knowledge in later centuries, not everyone was convinced mountain exploration was a sane idea. Even after climbers made several ascents of Mont Blanc, the highest peak in Europe, some felt "a large proportion of those who have made this ascent have been persons of unsound mind."[1]

Yet despite traditional attitudes, a few brave souls did venture into the mountains. Some sought to spread religion or to avoid religious persecution. Merchants looked for new trade routes and new markets. Others traversed unknown mountain ranges during migration and for colonization. Later pioneers simply wanted to extend the human knowledge of the world through science, discovery, and mapping. Whatever the reason, all of these early explorers forged a better understanding of and new relationships with mountains.

RELIGIOUS TRAVEL AND RITUAL

Some of the earliest climbers trekked mountains for religious purposes. In China, the monk Fa Xian, who lived between 350 and 422 CE, recognized there were a limited number of Buddhist scriptures available in the country. In order to access original texts to translate into Chinese, he needed to travel to India. Fa Xian and his companions traversed, but did not summit, the world's highest mountains, including those in the Hindu Kush, the Karakoram, and the Himalayas. In describing the crossing, Fa Xian asserted the mountains contained malicious dragons. He claimed that, if provoked, these dragons would spit "poisonous winds, rain, snow and even stones."[2] When Fa Xian returned to China 15 years later, with his vast collection of translated Buddhist texts, he opted to go by sea.

MOUNTAIN MYTH

Devil's Tower in Wyoming is a monolith, a massive, single chunk of rock. It rises 1,267 feet (386 m) above the plains and has been sacred to plains tribes since ancient times.[3] Ceremonial rituals are still performed there every year.

One popular legend about the origin of Devil's Tower comes from the Lakota Indians. The story recalls a day when a black bear approached seven young girls who were playing. Scared, the girls ran and jumped onto a low rock and pleaded for help from the rock. The rock heard them and rose upward, pushing the girls out of reach of the bear. Legend claims the visible grooves on the side of the tower were made by the bear clawing at the rock. As the bear clawed and jumped, the rock pushed the girls up farther into the sky. The girls are thought to be the seven stars of the Pleiades star cluster.

The laws that form the foundation of the Judeo-Christian tradition involve mountain climbing. The prophet Moses reportedly ascended Mount Sinai in Egypt, which was veiled in smoke "because the Lord had descended upon it in fire."[4] After 40 days and 40 nights, Moses came down the mountain carrying tablets containing God's written laws.

Mount Fuji is one of three holy mountains in Japan. The first recorded climb was in 633, and since then pilgrims have reached its top regularly. Today more than 100,000 people make the journey to the summit each year.[5] Buddhists and Hindus also make pilgrimages to holy mountains. The holiest mountain in Tibet is Mount Kailas. Each year, thousands of people travel in a clockwise direction around, rather than up, the mountain to gain enlightenment. To this day, the mountain remains unclimbed. Mountains also became the location for a growing number of Buddhist monasteries and temples throughout history.

In the Bible, Moses receives God's laws, the Ten Commandments, on Mount Sinai.

INCA OF THE ANDES

Numerous Incan sacrificial sites containing well-preserved mummies have been discovered in the Andes at elevations of more than 22,000 feet (6,750 m). Not only did the Inca perform religious ceremonies at high altitudes, but they also spent a great deal of their everyday lives at great heights. Between the mid-1400s and their defeat by the Spanish in 1532, the Inca created a vast, thriving civilization in the Andes Mountains. Many of their great cities were built at impressive altitudes, including their capital of Cuzco at 10,860 feet (3,310 m).[6] In addition, the Inca built a network of roads thousands of miles long. These roads crisscross the mountains, connecting the corners of the empire. The Inca also built terraces and aqueducts of stone into the mountains. More than any other ancient or modern culture, it appears the Inca were well adapted to the conditions and environment of mountain living. Scientists today are still puzzled by the Inca's ability to live and work at such high altitudes.

Incan priests climbed mountaintops in the Andes more than 500 years ago. The summits were used as altars where Incan priests sacrificed children in order to please their gods. In modern times, scientists and climbers have discovered several mummified bodies of these human sacrifices.

TRAVEL, RESOURCES, AND REFUGE

People have also traveled through the mountains during migration, for trade, to access resources, for refuge, and in times of war. In Asia, tradesmen moved salt from Tibet to India through the Himalayas in exchange for fabric and other goods. Likewise, the

Silk Road was a trade route through many countries and mountain ranges, used for centuries to transport goods from China to Europe and back. Most early mountain travel was done over a pass between mountains. When explorers began summiting mountains, it became necessary to walk along ridges to reach the peaks.

During the Second Punic War (218–202 BCE), military commander Hannibal of Carthage crossed the Alps in what some historians call one of history's "most improbable outflanking maneuvers."[7] The goal was to enter Rome from the north to launch surprise attacks. The Carthaginian army, commanded by Hannibal, assembled in Spain and journeyed toward Rome through the mountains. The army

THE SILK ROAD

One of the greatest trade routes in history was the Silk Road. From the 100s BCE until the end of the 1300s, it linked China and the Roman Empire. The Silk Road was actually a network of routes. Merchants and traders navigated these routes, which included travel through inhospitable deserts and the mountains of the Himalayas. People in the West were enamored with Chinese silk, but it was not the only ware traded along the route. Other items to reach the West included exotic animals, ceramics, and jade. Items transported in the other direction included gold and glass. The Silk Road also helped exchange culture between the East and the West.

included 50,000 foot soldiers, 9,000 soldiers on horse, and 37 elephants. Throughout the trek Hannibal and his army overcame surprise attacks, traps, slippery slopes, and steep and narrow passages through the mountains. After 15 days they emerged from the mountains. More than 30,000 of Hannibal's men had died.[8] Nonetheless, Hannibal's strategic approach proved effective. He and his army were able to inflict some of the worst defeats the Romans experienced during the war. While Carthage ultimately lost, Hannibal's alpine march remains one of the most famous military accomplishments in history that involved mountains.

Mountains were also used as refuges. In North America, ancestors of the Pueblo people used the mountains as a defensive strategy beginning in the 800s by building their village homes atop cliffs for safety. Later, their descendants excavated the sides of cliffs for their homes. Many of these

Hannibal led his army across the Alps.

Ascending Mont Aiguille's sheer slopes for the first time in 1492 was a tremendous feat that was not accomplished again for nearly 350 years.

dwellings are still visible today. In Nepal in the 1400s, several native groups retreated into the Himalayas to escape foreign invaders.

THE FIRST SUMMITERS

One of the earliest recorded recreational climbs was in the second century, when Roman emperor Hadrian climbed Mount Etna in Italy simply because he wanted to see the sunrise from the top. In 1336, the Italian poet Petrarch climbed Mont Ventoux in France "for the view."[9] Over the next several centuries, more and more people desired to see the world from atop a mountain.

The first recorded technical climb, in which ropes and other tools were used to assist the ascent, occurred in 1492 near Grenoble, France. Located there is Mont Aiguille, which had the nickname "unscalable mountain."[10] For reasons unknown, this mountain of sheer limestone walls captured the fancy of the king of France,

Today, Mount Pilatus has several paths leading to its summit, including a railway and stairs.

Charles VIII, and he ordered that it be climbed. Following the royal orders, Antoine de Ville assembled a team fit for the challenge. They took with them military equipment worthy of a full-scale siege of city walls, including ropes, ladders, rings, and grappling hooks. After reaching the summit, they stayed atop Mont Aiguille for three days, where de Ville erected the cross and banner of his king. No one was able to replicate de Ville's feat again until 1834.

In the century following the ascent of Mont Aiguille, naturalist Conrad Gessner popularized the idea of exploring mountains in their own right. While he originally explored the mountains as a botanist, he came to regard the mountain environment as a different world, describing the mountains as spiritual places. In 1555, he and his guides were the first people to reach the summit of Mount Pilatus in Switzerland. At the time, there was no established path. Instead, the group used alpenstocks, which are six-foot (2 m) wooden poles with iron-spiked tips, to navigate the difficult terrain to the summit. Gesner's writings about the ascent and other explorations are credited with encouraging others to explore greater heights.

In the 1700s, during the age of Enlightenment, people sought knowledge through all means, including adventures such as mountain climbing.

CHAPTER 3

SUMMITS, SCIENCE, SURVEYING, AND SIGHTSEEING

During the age of Enlightenment in the 1600s and 1700s in Europe, the reasons propelling mountain exploration shifted. The study of mountain environments developed in the Alps, and scientists and naturalists climbed mountains in search of knowledge. In North America, initial exploration of the West by settlers of European descent began.

HOW MOUNTAINS FORM

Earth's crust is made of massive, moving plates. Over time, plates can collide, buckle, fold, and lift. The most common type of mountain is a fold mountain, created when two plates collide and the earth's crust buckles upward, forming folds one on top of the other.

Fault-block mountains occur when faults or cracks in the earth's crust thrust blocks of rock upward and downward. The uplifted blocks become mountains.

Some mountains form when volcanoes erupt. Within volcanoes is a molten-hot mixture of liquid rock and gas called magma. Shifting and colliding plates underneath the volcano can cause the magma to push upward, and eventually the volcano erupts. Magma that spills onto the surface is called lava. Lava can pile up, creating a mountain. Dome mountains form when magma pushes upward on the surface of the earth but never erupts.

Finally, plateau mountains are flat, elevated areas pushed upward by Earth's internal shifting. Over time, weather and erosion shape plateau mountains.

SCIENTIFIC EXPLORATION

Early geologic thinking emphasized a biblical flood, or a similar catastrophe, as an explanation for Earth's surface features. One of the most notable scientists opposing the prevailing knowledge was James Hutton. Through his work and observations, Hutton recognized the formation of rock was not a result of a biblical flood, as most people believed. By the 1800s, scientists including Hutton came to understand processes such as erosion, which took place over long periods of time, were also involved. Scientists also developed the notion of the Ice Age, when slow moving glaciers covered large areas of Earth and carved landscapes.

Evidence Hutton collected suggested that Earth's rocks were part of "a continual process of geological compaction, erosion, and volcanic and tectonic activity."[1] Hutton's theories were innovative and challenged the prevailing beliefs that existed about the age and origin of the planet. As a result, he is known today as the father of modern geology.

The pursuit of knowledge was what initially attracted scientists to the mountains, but they were in awe once they began studying them. Horace-Bénédict de Saussure was a pioneer in the mountain sciences in the 1700s. Like Hutton, Saussure made countless scientific observations in the mountains.

GLACIOLOGY

Glaciology, the study of glaciers, saw significant advances during the early 1800s. Glaciers are slow-moving masses of ice that exist in many forms. Swiss glaciologist Franz Josef Hugi did not believe glaciers were unchanging as others did at the time. He set out to gather information proving their movement in 1827. He built a stone shelter on a glacier in Switzerland that served as his headquarters. Hugi drove stakes into the glacier and then carved marks into nearby rocks and measured the movement of the glacier over a series of three years. His work paved the way to the scientific world's understanding of glaciers.

His observations and experiments involved storms, barometric readings, the effects of altitude, and water depth and temperature of alpine lakes. Through his work, Saussure concluded the strata in rocks he found in the Alps were formed "by a process of compression of one new layer onto the next."[2] After visiting the alpine glacier Chamonix in 1760, Saussure wrote,

> *The majestic glaciers,*
> *separated by great*
> *forests and crowned by*
> *granite rocks which rise*
> *to incredible heights,*
> *offer one of the most*
> *magnificent and impressive*
> *sights imaginable.*[3]

These descriptive accounts, the work of scientists who studied mountains, and artists who

THE EVOLUTION OF ALPINE SCIENCES

Alpine sciences evolved during the age of Enlightenment. The scientists who studied the alpine environment made countless pioneering observations. Johann Jakob Scheuchzer was one such pioneer, and he made numerous trips in the Swiss Alps. In his recorded findings, Scheuchzer described rivers, lakes, springs, avalanches, and glaciers. He also drew detailed illustrations of plants, waterways, and minerals. Scheuchzer's contributions were instrumental in defining the alpine sciences including: botany (study of plants), geology (study of Earth's structure and origin), geophysics (physical Earth processes), glaciology (study of glaciers), mineralogy (study of minerals), paleontology (study of fossils), meteorology (study of weather), and cartography (mapmaking).

depicted them in their works during this time are credited with changing how Europeans thought about mountains. People no longer feared and avoided them. Instead, the mountains became respected places of exploration, inspiration, discovery, and beauty.

MONT BLANC: SCIENCE AND SPORT

In 1760, Saussure offered a reward to the first person to reach the 15,770-foot (4,807 m) summit of Mont Blanc, the highest peak in western Europe.[4] Saussure hoped a climber would find a route to the top so he himself might one day climb it to make scientific observations. Climbing a massive, icy mountain such as Mont Blanc was not undertaken lightly. Mountaineering presents a host of challenges and dangers, including exposure to extreme cold and risk of falling.

Several efforts to climb Mont Blanc for scientific purposes were made throughout the late 1700s. A doctor named Michel-Gabriel Paccard explored the mountain because of his interest in botany. Over several years, he

Balmat's revolutionary bivouac on Mount Blanc in 1775 opened the door to camping at high altitudes. This modern climbers' bivouac on the same mountain follows in his footsteps.

made numerous attempts to summit Mont Blanc. In 1786, Paccard met Jacques Balmat, who had made his own attempts to climb Mont Blanc in prior years. Paccard hired Balmat as his porter. On August 7 of that year, the pair began their ascent hauling their scientific equipment, a blanket, and alpenstocks, which were used for traction on snow and glaciers. Along the way, Paccard and Balmat used their alpenstocks as bridges over the mountain's crevasses. Balmat also carried an ax, which he used to hack into and grip ice. The going was tedious.

BIVOUACKING AND SUMMITTING

Mountain climbers often climb until nightfall, when they must decide to either descend or bivouac. Staying overnight at high altitudes is dangerous. Climbers avoided doing so prior to an unintended bivouac Balmat made back in 1775, which inspired future overnight stays. On an attempt on Mount Blanc that year, Balmat's fellow climbers retreated when faced with steep, icy slopes. Balmat continued upward. At dusk, he decided to retreat down the mountain, but he was caught in the dark. His overnight stay high on the mountain gave other climbers who heard of it confidence that it was possible, a feat they formerly thought of as too dangerous. While a breakthrough for climbers, high-altitude bivouacs are still a challenge to any

DANGERS OF THE COLD

Exposure to the cold is one risk climbers face. Serious damage or even death can be caused by prolonged exposure to the cold, and the risk of hypothermia or frostbite increases the closer climbers get to the summit. For every 1,000 feet (305 m) of elevation, the temperature drops 3 to 5 degrees Fahrenheit (2 to 3°C).

Hypothermia occurs when the body cannot stay warm. Symptoms include sleepiness, confusion, slurred speech, and clumsiness. Symptoms of hypothermia worsen the colder a person gets and will cause death if body temperature reaches 95 degrees Fahrenheit (35°C) or lower.

Frostbite occurs when a body gets so cold the blood vessels constrict. This reduces blood flow to extremities, such as fingers and toes, in order to keep blood flowing to vital organs. At the onset of frostbite, affected areas lose feeling and turn white or grayish-yellow. Skin and tissue freeze. Severe frostbite can result in permanent tissue damage and heightened sensitivity to cold. If frozen tissue dies, amputation of the affected areas is necessary.

mountaineer. At high altitudes, especially above tree line, water and shelter are scare. Exposed mountainsides are bitterly cold and susceptible to rapid changes in weather. Balmat awoke in the morning covered in frost, but he was able to descend and team up with Paccard years later with the goal of reaching the summit.

After bivouacking overnight during their 1786 climb, the pair rose at 4:00 a.m. By the afternoon of August 8, Paccard and Balmat faced the steepest, most exposed part of the route. Paccard had originally planned for them to bivouac for a second night, but there were no suitable sites, so the pair pressed on.

Paccard and Balmat reached the summit after 6:00 p.m. that day. Their ascent of Mont Blanc is credited as the formal beginning of mountaineering as a sport. Saussure reached the summit of Mont Blanc himself the following year, with Balmat as his guide.

EARLY NORTH AMERICAN EXPLORATION

In North America, mountain exploration was inspired not by science or sport, but by US interest in westward expansion. In 1803, the United States bought land from France, expanding the country. The land purchased was called the Louisiana Territory. It included a huge chunk of land west of the Mississippi River. Following the purchase, US President Thomas Jefferson commissioned a party to explore a route across the continent to the Pacific Ocean. Captain Meriwether Lewis was appointed to lead the expedition. He chose soldier and explorer

MOUNTAIN WEATHER

Mountains experience some of the most dangerous weather on Earth. Certain high peaks are even known to create their own weather. Conditions explorers face include rapidly changing weather, lightning, wind, snow, and rain. Shelter can be difficult to find in high elevations. It is important mountaineers have knowledge about and respect for mountain weather.

William Clark to assist him. Together they assembled a team of more than 30 men for the journey, which headed up the Missouri River in April 1804. After traveling up the river, the group acquired horses from a Shoshone village in order to cross the Rocky Mountains. Atop the mountains, the explorers did not see slopes leading down toward the Pacific, as they had hoped. Instead, as one member reported on September 18, 1805, "The mountains continue as far as our eyes could extend . . . much further than we expected."[5] The expedition members were the first white Americans to discover the immense size of the Rocky Mountains.

In addition to Lewis and Clark's team, another party was assembled to explore the southern part of the newly acquired Louisiana Territory. During a fall expedition in 1806, explorer Zebulon Pike observed from the eastern Colorado plains a mountain peak that towered above the rest. He set out to climb it with other members of his group. However, they did not have winter clothing and,

Explorer William Clark getting his first glimpse of the Rocky Mountains after several days, food was running low, so the explorers aborted their mission to climb the peak. Although Pike and his companions did not reach the summit, the peak was named in his honor: Pike's Peak.

The first known complete ascent of Pike's Peak was not until 1820, when US army major Stephen Long's expedition sought the source of the Platte River and came upon the mountain in their search. On July 14, after two days of climbing, expedition member Edwin James and two others summited Pike's Peak at 14,110 feet (4,301 m). It was the first documented ascent of any US peak higher than 14,000 feet (4,267 m).[6] However, some evidence exists that suggests American Indians may have reached the summit previously.

DRESSING FOR MOUNTAIN CLIMBING

Mountaineers must be prepared to face all kinds of extreme weather when climbing. Dressing in layers is key to staying safe and comfortable on mountains. It also allows climbers to add or shed layers easily depending on changing weather conditions. The layer next to one's skin is usually thin. It must pull moisture away from the body to keep the skin dry and prevent the body from cooling. Next is the insulating layer, which should trap warm air. This might include more than one piece of clothing, depending on conditions. Finally, the outer layer protects from wind, rain, and sun.

Exploration of the western United States continued into the 1800s. In 1842, explorer John Frémont sought a route through the Rocky Mountains. While navigating through the range, Frémont conducted a land survey and collected geographic and botanical data. He also ascended a peak that year in Wyoming, which was later named Fremont Peak after him. Between the years 1843 and 1844, Frémont also mapped the mountains of the Sierra Nevada. His discoveries and work are credited with influencing a wave of settlers to move West during this time.

ADVENTURE AND TOURISM

When Paccard climbed Mont Blanc, he hauled heavy equipment with him. Saussure and others likewise carted hefty apparatuses up steep slopes for scientific purposes. In the early 1800s, however, two brothers, Johann Rudolf Meyer and Hieronymus Meyer, claimed hauling scientific equipment up a mountainside "hampered a daring climber."[7] In 1811, the brothers set out to explore the Jungfrau summit, which reaches 13,642 feet (4,158 m) in the Bernese Alps, just for the sporting challenge.[8] They brought along no scientific equipment, packing only ropes, alpenstocks, and ladders. They also packed sufficient warm clothing and a large sheet to use as a tent. On August 3, Johann and Hieronymus reached the lower, secondary summit of the Jungfrau. The following year, Johann's son, Gottlieb Meyer, succeeded in reaching the highest summit. The family's expeditions in the Bernese Alps ushered in a new type of mountain climbing, done for fun and adventure.

The growth of tourism and travel in Europe in the 1800s facilitated the growth of climbing as a recreational activity. In 1821, the first mountain-climbing guide service in the world, the Company of Guides, was founded to assist tourists to Mont Blanc's peak. Guides were generally locals with climbing skills and knowledge of the mountains. They helped tourists navigate rocks and ice, carried equipment, carved steps in the ice, and interpreted fickle mountain weather, making their clients' adventures more pleasant. Guides were also hired to assist explorers and scientists up

A mountain guide carving steps into the ice during the late 1800s or early 1900s

the mountains. They helped their clients more easily ascend mountains and study them along the way.

Mountaineering equipment also advanced during this time. In the 1840s, the alpenstock and ax, which had become standard equipment used for mountain climbing, were combined to create the first ice ax. In the early 1860s, the idea was further developed. On the top of the pole was a flat, wide blade. Opposite that was a sharp pick. The result was a tool that climbers could use to halt a slide on steep sections and chop steps in the ice with the blade. The ice ax has continued developing over the decades and is still a critical tool for mountain explorers.

Mountaineering continued growing in popularity in the first half of the 1800s. In 1851, the sport received a publicist who

ALPINE GUIDES

Alpine guiding developed into a profession in the decades following the founding of the first climbing guide service. Two of the Alps' most famous guides were Christian Almer and Melchior Anderegg. Almer made several first ascents of peaks in the Alps with wealthy Victorian climbers. He is perhaps best known for attempting to beat Alfred Wills and his guides up the Wetterhorn, although Almer later joined forces with Wills's group and they ascended together. Almer's rival Anderegg was another top guide. Anderegg made numerous historic ascents in the Alps, including trekking a new, daring route up Mont Blanc.

championed exploration. Albert Smith was a writer who climbed Mont Blanc with an extensive entourage of guides and porters that year. The group carried with them an excessive amount food and drinks for the trip. After the climb, Smith produced a lively show full of anecdotes and songs describing his journey and presented it at the Egyptian Hall in Piccadilly, London. The show was such a success it ran for six years and made Smith a wealthy man. Mont Blanc was the only mountain Smith ever climbed, but his influence in popularizing mountaineering influenced future climbing culture.

MOUNTAIN ART AND LITERATURE

In the 1700s and 1800s, artists came to see mountains as places of inspiration, capturing the sense of grandeur, danger, and awe evoked by the mountains. Painter Caspar Wolf traveled into the Alps with scientific expeditions in the late 1700s. He portrayed the features of the landscapes up close, creating 200 oil paintings depicting the dramatic beauty of the mountains.

Writers of the romantic literary movement, including Samuel Taylor Coleridge, Percy Bysshe Shelly, and Lord Byron, wrote about the mountains and the emotions they incur. Shelly, for example, describes the feeling when first seeing the mountains as one "of ecstatic wonder not unallied to madness."[9]

The transcendentalist movement also drew public attention to nature. In 1836, Ralph Waldo Emerson's *Nature* promoted a new understanding and appreciation of nature and inspired Henry David Thoreau. Thoreau's writings about nature, including his most famous, *Walden*, are thought to have inspired the modern environmental movement.

Climbers in the Alps as the golden age of mountaineering was ending

CHAPTER 4

THE GOLDEN AGE OF MOUNTAINEERING

The golden age of mountaineering was ushered in with the 1854 ascent of the Wetterhorn by Englishmen Alfred Wills. The growing popularity of the sport, combined with expansion of the railroads, set the stage for unprecedented mountain exploration at that time. Between 1854 and 1865, 36 mountains in the Alps that were more than 13,000 feet (4,000 m) high were summited for the first time.[1]

MOUNTAINEERING CLUBS

At the time, the cost and time required to travel to a mountain range and then hire guides was something only the wealthy could afford. Early Alps mountaineers were mostly judges, landowners, clergymen, and businessmen with adequate incomes, and they were led up the mountains by professional guides. And most were British. Of the 36 first ascents higher than 13,000 feet (4,000 m) in the Alps, 31 were by British climbers.[2]

The first mountaineering club, the Alpine Club, was established in London, England, on December 22, 1857. It had 12 original members. Among them were the showman Smith, Wetterhorn climber Wills, and Alpine guidebook pioneer John Ball. By 1865, the club's professional, elite membership increased tenfold. Accounts of members' climbs were published in the *Alpine Journal* and "conveyed the zest of exploration and adventure, combined with a real sense of fun."[3]

Soon after the establishment of the Alpine Club, similar clubs emerged across Europe and then North America.

While the Alpine Club remained elitist, the other European clubs were not, and they grew more quickly. In addition to attracting members, these groups erected series of huts on the mountains for climbers. The Swiss Alpine Club built 38 such shelters by 1890. The French Alpine Club built 33. In North America, the first mountaineering club was the Appalachian Mountain Club, established in Boston in 1876. Its mission was to promote both climbing and stewardship of the mountains and surrounding areas of the Appalachian region. The Sierra Club, founded in 1892 by naturalist John Muir, similarly

MOUNTAINEERING BOOKS

Many climbers wrote of their experiences trekking the mountains in the 1800s. In 1856, Wills recounted the challenges and thrills of his climbs in *Wanderings Among the High Alps*. The Alpine Club's first president, John Ball, wrote guidebooks on the Alps' natural history and geography and guides describing equipment. Instructional books, such as *The Technique of Alpine Mountaineering*, published by the Swiss Alpine Club, kept climbers up to date on new techniques and equipment. In 1871, climber Edward Whymper published his memoir, *Scrambles Amongst the Alps*, which remains a mountaineering classic. The conclusion of the book reads,

Climb if you will, but remember that courage and strength are nought without prudence, and that a momentary negligence may destroy the happiness of a lifetime.[4]

encouraged members to "climb the mountains and get their good tidings."[5]

Over time, mountaineering attracted people from different social classes. Working-class men who lived in the Alps began climbing. Unburdened by travel, locals could explore the mountains at minimal cost. Likewise, they could readily access the mountains for a quick weekend adventure.

MATTERHORN

One of the most desirable peaks to climb in Europe was the Matterhorn, which stands at 14,692 feet (4,478 m) on the border between Switzerland and Italy.[6] By the mid-1860s, it was one of the only remaining great Alpine peaks that had not been summited.

English wood-engraver Edward Whymper was one of many obsessed with becoming the first to summit the Matterhorn. Whymper explored possible routes up the Matterhorn beginning in 1861. Over the next several years, he attempted to climb the mountain several times up the

Italian Ridge on the mountain's south side with various guides. Each time he was able to get a little higher, leaving Whymper feeling as if the peak were just out of reach.

Italian guide Jean-Antoine Carrel, whom Whymper had hired during previous ascents, was also racing to be the first to summit the Matterhorn. In 1865, Carrel declined to take Whymper up the Matterhorn again. Whymper approached guide Peter Taugwalder and Taugwalder's son Joseph to

THE SUMMIT OF THE MATTERHORN IN 1865 (NORTHERN END).

assist him. They teamed up with Whymper's former guide Michel Croz and Croz's clients as well. Among the seven that would make the ascent was also a relatively inexperienced climber named Douglas Hadow. Whymper had reservations about bringing Hadow along but was reassured that Hadow would be a good addition to the group.

The group departed on July 13, 1865, heading toward the Hörnli Ridge on the Swiss side of the Matterhorn. The seven bivouacked at 12,526 feet (3,818 m) and rose on the morning of July 14 to vie for the summit. The going was not as difficult as expected, but Hadow showed signs of exhaustion. Nonetheless, the group continued. Whymper and Croz reached the summit at 1:40 p.m. The others followed shortly after. When Whymper looked down the Italian ridge to the south, he saw Carrel's team just below.

Whymper and Joseph remained on the peak for one hour while the rest of the group started their descent, possibly to rest and enjoy their accomplishment. When

Whymper and members of the 1865 expedition on the summit of the Matterhorn

Whymper and the guide caught up to the main group, they were asked to rope themselves to the others because Hadow was struggling. The hope was in the event of a fall, Whymper and the others would act as anchors, preventing Hadow from plummeting. The group descended slowly, with Croz helping Hadow place his feet with each step. But Hadow slipped and the others heard Croz cry out.

Whymper saw the two men fall off the edge. Two others, attached to them by the rope, were yanked off with them. Whymper braced for the pull on the rope, but it snapped. Four of the seven climbers plunged to their deaths. Only Whymper and the Taugwalders survived.

The race to the summit of the Matterhorn had been one of

ROPES

During the golden age of mountaineering, ropes were made of natural fibers, most often hemp. Following the Matterhorn tragedy, the Alpine Club set standards for climbing ropes concerning strength and durability. Ropes that met the standards would have a thin red thread running their length. During World War II (1939–1945), synthetic ropes made of nylon were developed consisting of a core and a sheath. These ropes were less prone to freezing and crimps than ropes previously used, and the sheath protected the inner strands from wear. The new synthetic ropes also had more elasticity, lessening the chance the rope would snap if a climber fell or break a climber's ribs in a sudden stop. Ropes have continued advancing through the decades, becoming thinner and lighter.

the most public climbs to date. The tragedy that ensued also became a public spectacle. There were numerous inquiries into what had happened and outrage over the four senseless deaths.

Some people questioned if mountaineering was foolish. Among them was Great Britain's Queen Victoria. She had been shocked by the Matterhorn disaster and disapproved of mountain climbing because of its dangers. The queen inquired whether mountain climbing could be banned and contacted Prime Minister William Gladstone on the matter. Nothing ever came of the queen's inquiry, but new standards for the quality of ropes used in mountaineering were established. The summit and tragedy during descent signaled the end of the golden age of mountaineering. Whymper himself never climbed again in the Alps, although he did explore elsewhere.

RISE OF FEMALE MOUNTAINEERS

As the public outcry over the tragedy on the Matterhorn faded, mountain climbing actually increased in popularity.

Some female mountaineers maintained societal expectations by wearing skirts to climb—but the activity alone of their climbing often drew criticism.

Some women in Europe saw mountaineering as a form of social freedom. Cultural norms at the time dictated that women wear skirts, which presented both an inconvenience and a hazard while mountain climbing. Some, such as Elizabeth LeBlond, wore riding pants under their skirts. Once out of sight of the last hotel, LeBlond would remove the skirts for easier climbing. Still others fastened a rope between their legs, hitching up the skirt and creating pantaloons. English climber Mary Paillon simply wore men's clothing.

Another challenge facing female explorers was traveling with male companions. Not only was it seen as improper for women to sleep on mountainsides with men who were not their husbands, but also credit was usually given to the men for dealing with hardships. Men who climbed with women likewise put themselves at risk of social disapproval. Despite disapproval, women continued climbing. As more people became interested in climbing, many explorers began looking across borders for new mountain challenges.

FEMALE CLIMBERS

In 1808, mountain guide Jacques Balmat convinced Maria Paradis to climb Mont Blanc, believing the feat would boost Paradis's trade business of selling refreshments to climbers and tourists at the foot of the mountain. Paradis struggled on the climb, though, and only made it to the top with the assistance of Balmat and other guides. Despite this assistance, she became famous for being the first woman to summit Mont Blanc. However, because she was carried partway, another woman is sometimes considered the first to have actually climbed the mountain. Thirty years after Paradis's ascent, Henriette d'Angeville, an aristocrat from Geneva, Switzerland, planned her own ascent of Mont Blanc. In September 1838, d'Angeville hired a team of guides and porters and began her ascent. She summited fully under her own power.

Lucy Walker, known as the world's first accomplished female mountaineer, wore a billowy print dress on many of her 98 expeditions. In 1871, she became the first woman to reach the Matterhorn summit.

The Front Range stretches south from southeast Wyoming into central Colorado as part of the Rocky Mountains. This and other North American ranges saw increased exploration in the late 1800s.

CHAPTER 5

NEW FRONTIERS

With many of the major peaks in the Alps summited by the end of the golden age in 1865, mountain exploration in Europe altered course. Mountaineers began exploring more difficult routes, and some looked beyond the Alps for mountains that remained unexplored. In the United States, expeditions focused on both exploring new territory and summiting unclimbed peaks.

AMERICAN ASCENTS

In Colorado, there are 54 peaks higher than 14,000 feet (4,267 m).[1] Long's Peak, which dominates the Front Range horizon, was named after Stephen Long, who was the first American to discover the mountain in 1820. For many years after, climbers claimed the mountain could not be scaled. Following the ascent of the Matterhorn in Europe in 1865, there was a renewed urgency in the United States to summit Long's Peak. In 1868, a surveying party led by John Wesley Powell made it to the vast, flat top of the mountain on August 23. While this was the first recorded ascent, many believe American Indians likely climbed it beforehand.[2]

Further west, Muir explored the mountains of Yosemite and the Sierra Nevada beginning in 1868. His work as a writer and a conservationist led him to become one of the most influential people in US history. He is known as the "Father of Our National Parks" and founded the Sierra Club in 1892.[3]

INCREASED CHALLENGES

Following the golden age, many climbers sought new, more challenging routes up previously climbed mountains.

John Muir was especially fond of the Sierra Nevada mountain range, where a winding trail more than 200 miles (320 km) long was later named after him.

Early climbers sought the easiest route up the mountains, which often included climbing up snow and ice. This could be difficult, but it allowed steps to be cut. New climbers sought more difficult routes that included more vertical ascents, rock wall ascents, and exposed rock. One such challenge was the Brenva Face of Mont Blanc. The east-facing route was deemed one of the most daunting and technical walls in the Alps. Many thought it was impossible to climb. Still, Adolphus Moore aspired to climb it. He and his party, including guide Melchior Anderegg, set out on July 14, 1865. The complex ascent included climbing an icefall, navigating over a rocky buttress, and inching up a steep ice ridge. Despite these challenges, the group reached the summit on July 15.

DARING, DIFFICULT ASCENTS

Another climber seeking rockier, more difficult routes was Englishman Clinton Dent. For several

Modern climbers camping
beneath the exposed
rock of the Brenva Face of
Mont Blanc

of his climbs, he hired Swiss guide Alexander Burgener. Dent was determined to climb the Grand Dru, a spire of granite that towers above the Chamonix valley. Dent attempted to climb the Dru 18 times and failed each time. Finally, on the nineteenth attempt, in 1878, Dent, Burgener, and two others reached the summit.

Another emerging climber at the time was Albert Mummery. He began climbing in the 1850s, hiring guides and ascending peaks across the Alps. He followed Burgener, his guide, on a daring route up the Matterhorn. The morning of September 3, 1879, the two climbers worked their way up the Zmutt Ridge, which included maneuvering over a series of "rocky teeth."[4] The row of rock slabs covered with ice challenged the pair considerably. Nine hours after leaving the snowy ridge, they reached the peak.

NEW ALPINISM

As Mummery's abilities improved, he began climbing with friends instead of hired guides. Soon, Mummery and like-minded climbers no longer relied on the guides' knowledge and expertise to get them up a mountain. These explorers employed what became known as alpine-style climbing, trusting their own skills, carrying their own gear, carving steps in the snow and ice themselves, and fixing their own ropes. As Mummery stated after a climb without guides,

> *"This time we were without guides, for we had learnt the great truth that those who wish to really enjoy the pleasures of mountaineering must roam the upper snows trusting exclusively to their own skill and knowledge."*[5]

Many younger climbers even began climbing solo. Both climbing solo and climbing without guides was frowned upon by the Alpine Club, but the practices soon became

ALPINE-STYLE CLIMBING

Alpine style means doing more with less. It means carrying everything one needs on their own back and not relying on man-made, artificial aids.

Alpine-style climbers travel in small groups and carry only minimal food, water, gear, and bivouac equipment. With a lighter load, climbers can move more quickly. Mountaineers often push for the summit all at once and then descend. This is in stark contrast to previous summit bids that involved numerous companions and tons of food and equipment. On those expeditions, supplies and climbers are gradually shuttled up the side of the mountain through a series of camps until in a position for a team to make a summit bid.

Climbing in small groups without a guide and with climbers carrying all supplies on their backs characterizes alpine climbing, which is still popular today.

commonplace among Europe's greatest climbers. Also adding to the new challenge of climbing was the notion of traveling "fast and light."[6] Mummery helped to pioneer the idea of carrying little and moving quickly.

At the same time, technology for climbers had improved significantly, including metal pegs called pitons and crampons, pieces of metal with piercing spikes on the bottom that strap on to a climber's shoe. These new inventions revolutionized climbing but also opened the door to the debate over the proper way to

EARLY PITONS AND CRAMPONS

A piton is a metal peg with a loophole on one end. Climbers hammer them into a crack in a rock, clip a carabiner into the piton hole, and run a rope through the carabiner. Ropes are threaded through the holes to make climbs safer. Austrian and Italian climbers developed the use of pitons and carabiners, while English climbers such as Mummery felt they were cheating and shunned their use. Piton use increased and evolved, and they are still widely used today.

In 1876, the first full-boot crampon was developed. The device initially had six points on the bottom for gripping slippery surfaces without needing to carve in steps.

ACCLIMATIZATION

Acclimatization is crucial to a climber's success at high altitude. The air density at 18,000 feet (5,486 m) is half that at sea level, so the body has to work harder to get enough oxygen.[9] The air contains the same percentage of oxygen at high altitude as at sea level, which is 21 percent.[10] The difference is that at a high altitude, there is less air pressure, meaning the same physical amount of air contains oxygen molecules that are more spaced out. A physical breath takes in the same spatial amount of air, but there are less oxygen molecules in it. Because of this, the lungs get less oxygen with each breath.

Thus climbers take steps to acclimatize, including staying hydrated and setting a slow, even pace. Climbers also use a technique known as the rest step. They move in small steps, stopping with each step for a second or two, giving weary, oxygen-deprived muscles a short break. Climbers also practice pressure breathing by breathing forcefully and frequently to keep the body's oxygen levels higher.

climb a mountain. Many embraced the latest improved equipment. Others saw climbing with aids as being against the "pure" style of climbing without.[7] Mummery best described the new generation of climbers when he said the spirit of mountaineering lay "not in ascending a peak, but in struggling with and overcoming difficulties."[8]

BREATHING DIFFICULTIES

In 1880, Whymper traveled to the Ecuadorian Andes to study the effects of altitude sickness on the human body. He hired his Matterhorn rival Carrel to accompany him. Whymper made the first ascent of numerous peaks there, including the volcano Mount Chimborazo, which is 20,702 feet (6,310 m) high.[11]

Many explorers have studied the effects of high altitude on the body. Altitude sickness can begin at elevations as low as 5,000 feet (1,524 m).[12] Symptoms include headache, nausea, vomiting, difficulty sleeping, dizziness, and fatigue.

In 1894, Mummery traveled to the Himalayas to explore Nanga Parbat in Pakistan, the ninth-highest mountain in the world at 26,660 feet (8,126 m).[13] The towering mountain is the westernmost peak in the Himalayas, and one of the most accessible. As was his style at the time, Mummery traveled simply up the mountain with his friends. They approached the mountain from several routes, all unexplored. Although Mummery did not feel the effects of altitude at 19,000 feet (5,791 m), the others did, and the group eventually descended.

FEATS OF ALPINE CLIMBING

When Mummery attempted Nanga Parbat, he did so in alpine-style climbs. Such an undertaking was revolutionary. Although his climbs were not successful, Mummery was far ahead of his time in the mountaineering world. An explorer did not accomplish an alpine climb up a peak approximately 26,250 feet (8,000 m) until 1975.

The risk of avalanche increases following a snowstorm, especially if fresh snowfall accumulates more than 12 inches (30.5 cm).

Mummery attempted Nanga Parbat again in 1895 with two companions who were hired to accompany him. After they set out on August 24, the trio was never seen again. One theory is that they were victims of an avalanche, which is a constant threat to climbers ascending snowy peaks. Despite the mystery surrounding Mummery's disappearance, his exploratory steps into the Himalayas foreshadowed the future of mountain exploration.

AVALANCHES

Avalanches are the result of several factors. The integrity of snow layers, air temperature, steepness of a slope, wind, and more can all combine to create avalanche conditions. The most common avalanches occur when a large slab of snow separates from the mountain. The snow then breaks apart and races downhill. Within five seconds, snow can travel as fast as 81 miles per hour (130 kmh), giving those in its path little time to escape.[14] In the event of an avalanche, victims in the snow can make swimming motions, essentially trying to keep themselves floating on the surface as the snow descends. Once it stops, however, the snow hardens, almost similar to concrete. For those buried, movement and self-rescue are almost impossible—they can only hope for a companion to shovel them out.

EXPLORER IN FOCUS
ALBERT MUMMERY

Albert Mummery was an unlikely mountaineer. Born in 1855, he was a sickly child. Nonetheless, Mummery grew stronger as he aged and began climbing in 1871. His passion grew quickly. On the mountains, Mummery was strong, agile, and strategic. He could not, however, carry heavy loads, due to a weak spine. Thus Mummery developed lighter equipment and more efficient techniques, becoming an innovator in mountaineering. He wrote an influential climbing book in 1895 titled *My Climbs in the Alps and Caucasus.* He was respected by many fellow climbers.

Early European climbers such as Mummery greatly underestimated the challenges involved in climbing the Himalayas, thinking of the range as a larger Alps. New approaches to expeditionary mountaineering would need to be introduced and used in the Himalayas before mountaineers were able to climb the big peaks.

Climbers take in the Longuta Glacier and the Caucasus Mountains, where unexplored, hard-to-reach peaks drew several explorers in the 1880s.

CHAPTER 6

NEW PEAKS

As mountaineers sought fresh territory to explore in the late 1800s, they traveled further. At the time, the Caucasus Mountains in western Russia were difficult to access and explore. The journey across Europe took eight days on a train and more than two days on a pony. Yet for those that made the trip, the Caucasus Mountains provided endless wild, unexplored territory. Dent, Moore, Burgener, and other climbers, as well as Mummery before he was lost in the Himalayas, made the journey to explore the region, each making numerous first ascents and traverses.

79

One of the first to launch a systematic expedition into the Karakoram Range in Pakistan was Martin Conway in 1892. The Karakoram Range is part of the larger Himalayan chain, which is 150 miles (240 km) across in places. Conway's goal was to survey and map the Karakoram, including the glaciers. He ultimately mapped 2,000 square miles (5,180 sq km) of the region, setting the stage for future large-scale expeditions of the area.

Travel became more accessible to people as technology progressed. At the turn of the century and into the first decade of the 1900s, the Americas became a magnet for climbers wanting to explore untouched mountains.

NORTH AND SOUTH AMERICA

One previously unexplored peak in South America was Aconcagua. The eroding volcano is the tallest in the Americas at 22,831 feet (6,959 m).[1] It sits

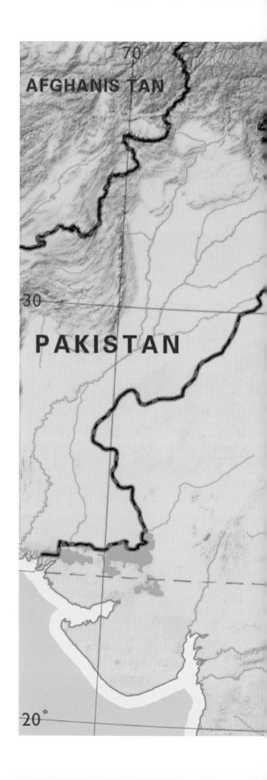

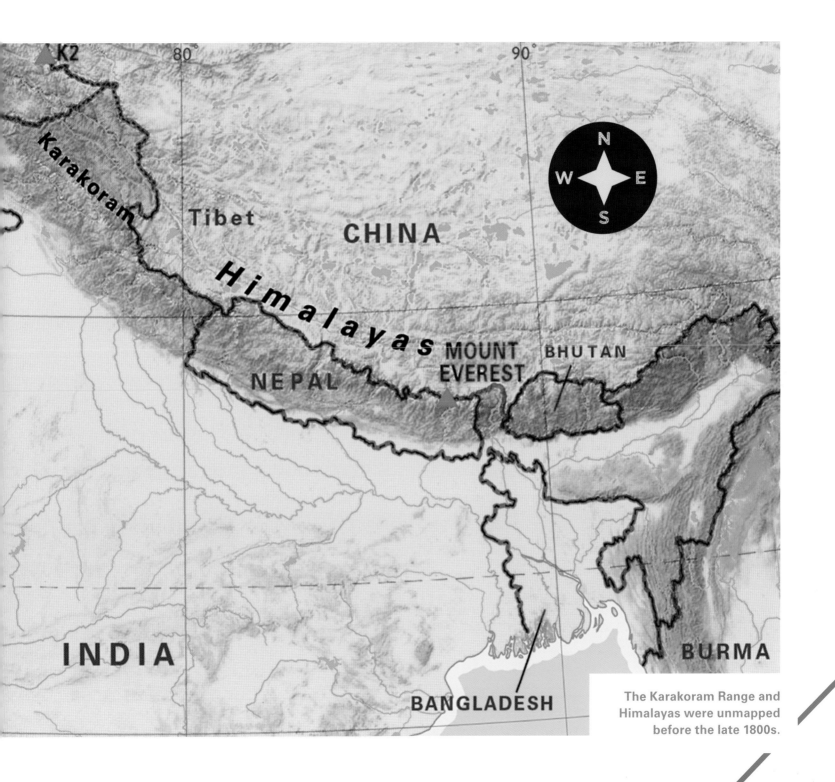

K2

80°

90°

Karakoram

Tibet

CHINA

N
W E
S

H i m a l a y a s

MOUNT EVEREST

BHUTAN

NEPAL

INDIA

BURMA

BANGLADESH

The Karakoram Range and Himalayas were unmapped before the late 1800s.

in west-central Argentina near the border with Chile. In the late 1800s, Aconcagua remained unclimbed, as far as anyone knew. Matthias Zurbriggen was a Swiss guide and renowned explorer at the time, and he was hired frequently by Englishman Edward FitzGerald. Zurbriggen journeyed to South America in 1896 to guide FitzGerald to Aconcagua's summit. Approximately 6,000 feet (2,000 m) from the top, FitzGerald succumbed to the extreme cold and the altitude and could not go on. FitzGerald agreed to allow Zurbriggen to continue alone. Zurbriggen summited solo on January 14, 1897.

Exploration also increased in North America at the turn of the century. In 1902, prominent climbers and conservationists founded the American Alpine Club (AAC). Similar to the Andes, the Canadian Rockies offered explorers a considerable expanse of untouched mountains. Facilitated by the Canadian-Pacific Railway, climbers began to make the journey to North America to explore the range.

The man credited with leading the exploration of the Canadian Rockies was an Austrian guide named Conrad

Kain. After gaining experience in the Alps and earning a good reputation as a guide, Kain began leading expeditions in Canada. There he made dozens of first ascents in the Canadian Rockies and in the more technical Bugaboos in British Columbia, Canada, which required more gear and more skill. In 1913, Kain and two companions were the first to climb the Canadian Rockies' highest peak, Mount Robson, at 12,972 feet (3,954 m).[2]

MOUNT MCKINLEY

The highest mountain in North America, Mount McKinley, was also summited in 1913. The higher of Mount McKinley's two summits, the South Summit, is

AMERICAN ALPINE CLUB

Among the founders of the American Alpine Club (AAC) were the club's first president Charles Fay and several successful female climbers including Annie Smith Peck and Fannie Bullock Workman. The club's second president was conservationist John Muir. Under his leadership, the AAC evolved from a club of the social elite to one more focused on environmental conservation.

According to the AAC's mission statement, the club sponsors climbing expeditions and focuses on safety and survival at high altitudes, environmental policy, and advancements to climbing equipment and clothing, among other things. Since its inception, the AAC has worked with the US Forest Service and the National Park Service to balance use of natural resources with wilderness protection. It has also been a part of historic expeditions to previously unexplored regions across the globe, even negotiating access into politically restricted regions around the world.

20,320 feet (6,194 m) high.[3] The mountain is also known as Denali, and it sits in the Alaska Range. Exploration of this mountain posed challenges to explorers of the same magnitude as mountains in the Himalayas. Not only is Mount McKinley extremely remote, but it also rises more than 18,000 feet (5,500 m) above the tundra, which is the open, mainly flat area, creating an abrupt vertical climb for mountaineers.[4] In addition, Mount McKinley is one of the coldest mountains on Earth outside of Antarctica and prone to some of the world's worst weather.

American Frederick Cook made the first attempts to summit Mount McKinley in the early 1900s. His exploration took him 400 miles (644 km) from the coast toward the mountains. He traversed swamps and tundra and battled mosquitoes. Cook was ultimately defeated by Mount McKinley on two separate attempts.

A caribou grazes in front of Mount McKinley in Denali National Park.

Yet he faked a summit photo and returned home to give false accounts of his accomplishment.

The lower, North Summit of Mount McKinley was reached in 1910 by a trio of Alaskan miners known as the Sourdough Expedition. Then in 1913, an English clergyman living in Fairbanks, Alaska, put together a team. Starting out in the winter in order to be on the mountain by early summer, the team painstakingly hauled loads up the mountain. Along the way, they stocked different camps. They shot caribou for food. The group struggled in both heat and cold, and they had trouble breathing in the thin air of the high elevation. After 50 days, they reached Mount McKinley's summit.

DENALI VS. MCKINLEY

The name Denali means "high one" or "great one" in the indigenous language of its surrounding Alaskan area.[5] However, the peak is also known by another name. In the late 1800s, a gold prospector named the peak Mount McKinley in honor of the sitting US president, William McKinley.

The name Mount McKinley was the mountain's official name until the 1970s. At that time, the Alaska Board of Geographic Names officially reestablished the peak's original name, Denali. To this day, however, the US Board on Geographic Names still recognizes Mount McKinley as the official name of the mountain.

GREATER HEIGHTS, GREATER RISK

As mountaineers explored greater heights, the lack of oxygen became a greater issue for them. Many early climbers experienced hypoxia, which is a lack of oxygen to the body's vital organs.

Over time, many scientists and explorers studied and experienced firsthand the effects of altitude on the human body. Besides Mummery, one of the first explorers to research the effects of altitude was Scottish chemist Alexander Kellas. During his lifetime, Kellas joined several expeditions to the Himalayas and was the first to systematically study acclimatization effects. Kellas himself also made several first ascents in the range in the early 1900s and reached heights previously unattained. He also developed two different systems to provide oxygen for climbers at high altitude. One stored pressurized oxygen in heavy steel cylinders. The weight was a hindrance to climbers. The other produced its own oxygen through a chemical reaction. However, the climber had to be resting in order for the system to operate properly.

Kellas's published work on altitude initiated a debate over whether Everest could be summited without oxygen. Kellas was part of the first expedition to Everest in 1921, but he died along the way. It would not be the last team to tackle the towering peak or the last to experience tragedy in its heights.

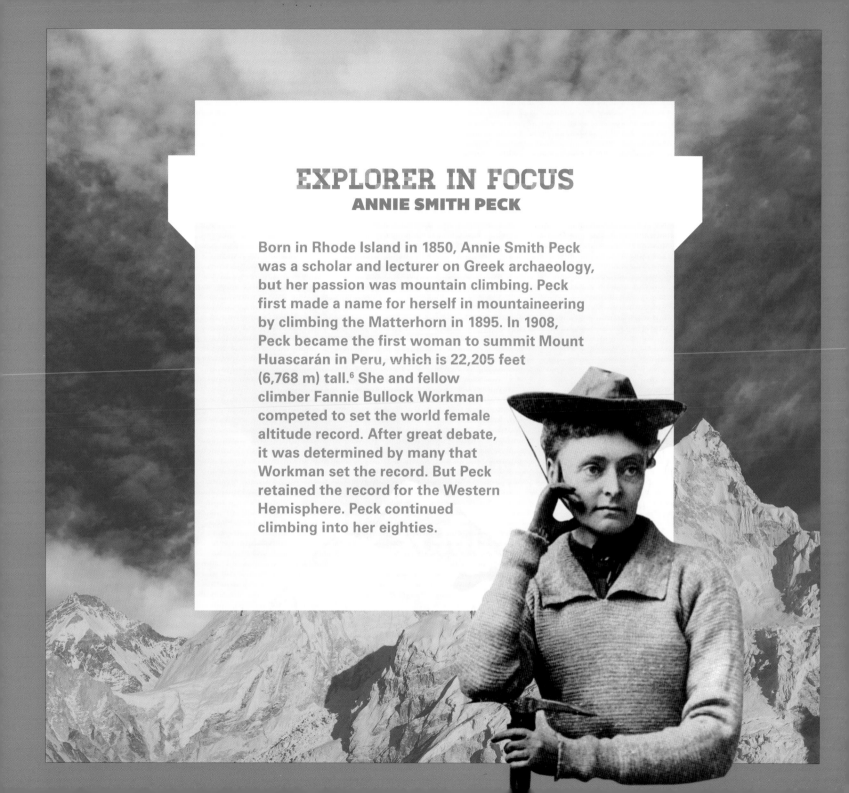

EXPLORER IN FOCUS
ANNIE SMITH PECK

Born in Rhode Island in 1850, Annie Smith Peck was a scholar and lecturer on Greek archaeology, but her passion was mountain climbing. Peck first made a name for herself in mountaineering by climbing the Matterhorn in 1895. In 1908, Peck became the first woman to summit Mount Huascarán in Peru, which is 22,205 feet (6,768 m) tall.[6] She and fellow climber Fannie Bullock Workman competed to set the world female altitude record. After great debate, it was determined by many that Workman set the record. But Peck retained the record for the Western Hemisphere. Peck continued climbing into her eighties.

A climber scales a rocky mountain face in the Italian Dolomites in 1910.

CHAPTER 7

GREATER CHALLENGES

In the decades before World War I (1914–1918), climbing techniques and devices continued advancing. At the time, many older climbers did not approve of the increased use of the artificial climbing aids. Nonetheless, the younger generation, armed with ambition and technology, aimed to get off the ridges and begin climbing faces, which could be riskier. Ridges offer the advantage of a direct route to the summit, with less chance of being hit by avalanche.

NORTH FACES

In the Northern Hemisphere, rock walls that face north are shadowed and chilly. This presents climbers with not only physical challenges, but with psychological ones as well. Three of the greatest north walls in the Alps are the Matterhorn, the Grandes Jorasses, and the Eiger. The north face of the Matterhorn rises 3,330 feet (1,015 m) and includes a slanted couloir, or deep gully, and a "vertical-to-overhanging rock wall."[1] Two brothers who tackled this face arrived in the town of Zermatt, at the base of the mountain, by bicycle in 1931. From there, Toni and Franz Schmid worked up the first ice slope. The next day, after working their way up a complicated, previously unclimbed route, they were the first to summit the mountain by that face.

Among climbers, the competition to be the first to ascend the north faces intensified. The north face of Grandes Jorasses, in the Mont Blanc massif, was attempted several times. In the summer of 1935, Rudolf Peters and Martin Maier embarked on an ascent of what today is known

A modern climber ascends the Croz Spur route up the steep, shadowy north face of Grandes Jorasses, which continues to challenge climbers today.

as the Croz Spur. They bivouacked below the peak's first rock tower. As they cooked their meal, they were hit by a rock fall, destroying their cooking equipment. Despite this, the pair climbed up to the Second Tower. Peters and Maier moved quickly over the ice field, due, in part, to their use of advanced ten-point crampons with front spikes. The new crampons had been developed in 1908 by Oscar Eckenstein, innovating earlier designs. A second rock fall occurred, and Maier was mildly injured. But the pair was still not deterred, and they reached Croz Spur's summit at 8:00 p.m. in the evening, making camp atop the peak.

Another challenging climb is the north face of the Eiger in Switzerland, also known as the Eigerwand or Killer Wall. It is a 6,000-foot (1,828 m) vertical climb.[2] The route includes several challenging formations, such as overhangs, chimneys, and a funnel-shaped snowfield called the White Spider, which acts like a chute during avalanches and with rock fall.

Prior to 1938, climbers made several attempts to climb the

ESCAPING MOUNTAIN DEATHS

On a mountain, the simplest injury or illness can become fatal due to the inaccessibility of medical care. Getting too cold can quickly lead to death. A basic tenet among climbers is "never underestimate the mountain and always be prepared."[3]

If mountaineers become seriously hurt or sick, they have to be evacuated. This task usually falls to others in one's group, illustrating the importance of climbing with trusted, experienced companions. In the era of satellite phones and radios, accessing additional resources is easier. Still, the patient must be taken to a place others can easily reach. And, given the remoteness and terrain on which mountaineers travel, a rescue is hazardous in and of itself.

An updated version of the 12-point crampons developed in the 1930s is still used by climbers today to ascend icy mountainsides.

Eigerwand. During that time, the face claimed several lives. The first pair, from Germany, made it two-thirds of the way up the wall in 1935. One of their bodies was spotted two weeks later from an airplane, frozen in the upright position on a ledge. Today climbers still refer to that spot as the "Death Bivouac."[4] In 1936, two Austrians and two Bavarians teamed up for another attempt. None of the four survived. Another death occurred on the Eigerwand in 1937. Then, in 1938, Germans Anderl Heckmair and Ludwig Vörg took on the challenge with a variety of ice pegs and the recently developed 12-point crampons. These have two additional points that point forward from the toe to allow a climber to kick into snow or ice. Partway up, Heckmair and Vörg met a

Mountain climbing equipment from 1945, including hammer, ax, crampons, and iron spikes

pair of Austrians, and together the foursome continued their quest, with Heckmair in the lead. After several overnight bivouacs, storms, and harrowing falls, the group summited on July 24, 1938. The men were heralded as heroes, especially Heckmair, who was thought to be a climbing genius and a man of unparalleled skill. The north face of the Eiger had proved to be a climb of extreme technical difficulty, requiring significant skill and experience, and mastering it altered the course of mountaineering.

NEW TECHNOLOGY

New techniques evolved in the early 1900s that used more pitons than in the past. Some used pitons and rope only for protection from falling and not to pull themselves up the mountain. Others used pitons and ropes to actually pull themselves up the mountain, rather than relying on their hands and feet only. The use of the soft steel pitons accelerated amidst debates over whether their use was "fair means."[5] Following World War II (1939–1945), innovators forged a hard steel piton. This new development led to accelerated use on large rock walls, despite concerns that the pitons, which could not be removed once hammered into the rock, marred the mountains climbers loved so much.

Ice screws were also an essential development. By screwing the device into the ice, vertical ice climbs became possible. Other technology that became available and evolved following World War II included nylon ropes; clothing that better protected climbers from cold, wind, and rain; and more apparatuses to aid and protect climbers, such as screws, winches, carabiners, and harnesses. As equipment continued developing, so did climber's interests in ascending new peaks.

YOSEMITE

Yosemite National Park in California caught the eye of ambitious climbers following World War II. With its enormous and previously unclimbed granite walls, climbers of all nationalities flocked to the park with innovative gear.

MILITARY MOUNTAIN TRAINING GROUNDS

During World War II, the US Army sought a mountain training ground for soldiers to prepare them for the fight in the mountains of Europe. They turned to the Colorado Rockies. Camp Hale was established in the Eagle River Valley, and in December 1942, more than 11,000 troops were sent there to train. Men of the 10th Mountain Division trained for two years in conditions similar to those found in the Alps to prepare them for war abroad. The soldiers perfected skiing techniques, adjusted to the altitude, learned to battle the cold, and more. The training was relentless. In January 1945, the 10th Mountain Division traveled to Italy, where they were instrumental in several battles, including those in Monte Castello, Monte Belvedere, and Monte della Torraccia. Today there is a series of huts for backcountry skiers and hikers in the Rockies named in honor of the 10th Mountain Division.

El Capitan's towering granite walls reflect in the Merced River in Yosemite National Park.

Prior to technological advancement in climbing gear, climbing the vertical walls in Yosemite, such as Half Dome and El Capitan, was unimaginable. In 1957, armed with enough gear and rope to rescue themselves if necessary, Royal Robbins set out to climb the face of Half Dome with

ROCK CLIMBING

Rock climbing has its roots in mountaineering. In the 1950s, as technology improved, rock climbing became its own sport.

Rock climbers continued developing pitons and bolts and also developed nuts and camming devices to aid their climbs. Nuts are wedges made of metal that have wire looped through one end. They are shoved into tight rock cracks and used to hold secure what is attached to the wire. Camming devices are also inserted into cracks, but rather than being wedged, as nuts are, they are spring-loaded and expand into a crack to grip it, and therefore secure the ropes attached to it. With these advancements came increasing concerns about damaging the rock. Thus began a "clean climbing" campaign to stop the use of hammering pitons and drilling for bolts.[7] Over time, better rock climbing devices that were easier on the rock and easier to use were developed, allowing rock climbers the possibility of forging new routes up more difficult faces.

two other climbers. The climb included maneuvering up blank faces without cracks and past large overhangs. They had to bivouac on ledges for four nights, and they finally reached the top on the fifth day. The feat pioneered climbing in Yosemite.

Not to be outdone, climber Warren Harding looked up the side of El Capitan. Soaring above him was the Nose, a vertical wall of granite approximately 3,000 feet (900 m) high.[6] The logistics of such a challenge would have intimidated a lesser climber. Harding approached the face as if it were an expedition. He fixed ropes, hammered pitons into the cracks in the rock, drilled holes to screw in bolts, and created makeshift camps where he and his team would bivouac. The team climbed up and down to resupply throughout the summer of 1957. They continued further up the mountain on each ascent, but went home in winter. Harding and his team returned in the summer of 1958 and started up their previously established route. Harding fixed more anchors but had to leave the mountain during tourist season at the request of park rangers. In the fall he returned and tackled the most daunting sections. Finally, after 45 days on the face, spread out over 18 months, Harding achieved what no one thought possible—he made it to the top of the Nose.

Harding's achievement was masterful, but it relied heavily on fixed equipment. He drilled 125 bolt holes and placed more than 600 pitons. This fueled the debate over the ethics of such an approach. Others contemplated approaches with less gear up more natural systems of cracks. In 1961, Robbins and a team climbed the Nose in just six days. They only drilled 13 bolt holes. The conflicting philosophies of mountaineering equipment would continue.

Certain cultures regard their peaks as religiously significant. Buddhists decorate Everest with prayer flags. To retain climbing privileges, climbers must respect cultural beliefs and rules concerning exploration.

CHAPTER 8

TOP OF THE WORLD

Mummery's 1895 expedition into the Himalayas in Pakistan was the first of hundreds before World War II. The teams that embarked on these journeys traveled into the unknown. They were challenged not only by the vastness of the ranges but also by the travel distance to the base of the mountains: while approaching, they contended with tropical forests, river rapids, rock slides, and icefalls. Additionally, there were political barriers to deal with as well. Climbing in foreign countries requires permission and permits, which can be difficult for foreigners to obtain. In the Himalayas, once foreign climbers were granted access to mountains, they often employed local Sherpas to guide them. Sherpas respect the mountains and are familiar with the terrain. Many Sherpas have turned mountaineering into a career.

HEIGHTENED CHALLENGE

Once in the Himalayas, perhaps the greatest obstacle facing all climbers is altitude. Being 26,247 feet (8,000 m) above sea level is near the edge of a human's ability to survive. This height is called the Death Zone because of reduced air pressure. As a result, it is difficult to get enough oxygen. Climbers describe it as a "walk along the knife-edge between life and death."[1] Despite the dangers of the Death Zone, explorers pushed past it to even higher

SHERPAS

The Sherpa people of the Himalayas originated in Tibet, and many migrated to Nepal more than 400 years ago. When large European climbing expeditions arrived in the Himalayas, they quickly realized the Sherpas' familiarity with the mountain, and they employed Sherpas as porters. Many Sherpas have emerged as experienced, skilled mountaineers. Tenzing Norgay and Ang Tharkay are among the most famous and accomplished.

Sherpas earn a substantial living being a part of expeditions. The money supports individual families, and the region has been able to invest in hospitals and schools as a result of Everest's popularity.

heights. On a June 1924 expedition to Everest in Tibet, two men reached a height of approximately 28,117 feet (8,570 m). During that same expedition, climbers George Mallory and Andrew "Sandy" Irvine also made a high ascent, although their highest point remains unknown. They never returned to camp. Numerous search expeditions were mounted through many decades. Mallory's body was discovered in 1999, but Irvine's remains lost.

In 1934, British climbers Bill Tilman and Eric Shipton teamed up in search of a possible route to the top of 25,643-foot (7,816 m) Nanda Devi in the Indian Garhwal Himalayas.[2] Nanda Devi is extremely difficult to reach, as it is surrounded by a ring of other mountains all more than 21,000 feet (6,400 m) high. Tilman and Shipton went on a lightweight pioneering expedition and succeeded in being the first to explore the Nanda Devi Basin, also known as the Nanda Devi Sanctuary. In 1936, Tilman returned and summited Nanda Devi with another British climber, Noel Odell, the last man to see Mallory and Irvine alive on

Everest. They did so without supplementary oxygen. It was the highest summit ever reached at that point in history.

Himalayan exploration ceased during World War II. After the war, it became a matter of national pride to see which country's teams would be the first to summit one of the world's 14 peaks higher than 26,247 feet (8,000 m). Climbers took advantage of wartime lessons. Expeditions were planned and strategized in the same manner as military campaigns. Climbing technology had advanced during the war, and mountaineers took advantage of the latest equipment, including oxygen apparatuses.

Also following the war, Nepal opened its borders to foreign

PREPARING TO CLIMB THE WORLD'S HIGHEST PEAKS

Expeditions to the world's highest mountains are undertakings that take years of planning and preparation. Before considering such an endeavor, a climber must gain experience with altitude and cold and practice technical skills. Getting physically fit is also critical.

Those traveling to foreign countries must secure visas, passports, and immunizations. Permits are needed to climb in some places. Travel arrangements need to be made, including flights and ground transportation to towns and villages nearest to the mountain.

A week or so prior to the trip, climbers assemble and pack clothing, equipment, and food, which itself is a skill. Every item must be evaluated for its weight and usefulness. Climbers must also find a balance between being prepared and over packing.

climbers for the first time. Eight of the world's 26,247-foot (8,000 m) peaks lie on the border or within Nepal, so this decision provided climbers great opportunity. The French put together a team to explore the Himalayas from the Nepalese side. The leader was experienced climber Maurice Herzog. Climber Louis Lachenal and six others accompanied him. Their original goal was to summit Dhaulagiri, the seventh-highest peak on Earth at 26,795 feet (8,167 m).[3] After weeks of pushing through previously unexplored territory, Herzog decided their best chance for a summit was instead Annapurna at 26,545 feet (8,091 m).[4] With the monsoon season fast approaching, the team employed Sherpas and raced up Annapurna. On June 3, 1950, after a grueling couple of weeks, Herzog and Lachenal succeeded in summiting the mountain. However, their glory was quickly overshadowed by a grueling descent. The miserable trek took days, challenged by storms, cold, and mud. Both men suffered frostbite, and Herzog lost all his fingers and toes.

EXPEDITION IN FOCUS
MOUNT EVEREST, 1924

In June 1924, Noel Odell, a geologist on the Everest expedition, watched from below as climbers George Mallory and Sandy Irvine approached the Second Step, near the base of Everest's summit pyramid, and climbed out of sight. As Odell watched, clouds enveloped the mountain. No one saw Mallory or Irvine again.

Mallory, a highly revered climber both then and now, was on his third British expedition to Everest. Irvine had no high-altitude climbing experience but was skilled at fixing oxygen apparatuses.

To this day, whether or not the two reached the summit of Everest remains a mystery. Some believe Mallory and Irvine's route would have been impossible for them because climbing the rock outcrop of the Second Step requires fixed ropes, anchors, and a ladder, which they did not carry with them. Some speculate Mallory and Irvine did indeed summit and were descending after sunset.

Mallory's body was discovered in 1999 with his snow goggles in his pocket. Irvine's body has yet to be recovered. Some believe the camera he carried would solve the mystery once and for all.

Mallory, *left*, and Irvine, *right*, at their camp on Everest in June 1924, the last time either were captured alive on film

LHOTSE
27,840 ft.

CAMP 7
27,550 ft.

CAMP 6
25,840 ft.

CAMP 5
22,630 ft.

WESTERN CWM

NUPTSE
25,680 ft.

CAMP 4
21,150 ft.

CAMP 3
19,350 ft.

ICE FALL

CAMP 2
18,370 ft.

CAMP 1
17,220 ft.

KHUMBA GLACIER

BASE CAMP

THE QUEST FOR EVEREST

Over the next couple of years, climbers searched for a route up Everest's 29,035-foot (8,850 m) summit. In 1952, the Swiss reached 28,215 feet (8,600 m), but ran out of energy and supplies before they could summit. Then, in 1953, the British organized an expedition to the Himalayas. Colonel John Hunt was appointed the team's leader. Known for his strong leadership and planning and organizational skills, Hunt orchestrated the expedition route and chose team members strategically.

Among the group were Tenzing, a Sherpa from Nepal, and Hillary, a New Zealander. Tenzing was born within miles of Everest, and over time he developed a driving ambition to summit the highest mountain on Earth. By the age of 19, Tenzing had made a name for himself among the world's best climbers. He worked for Shipton in 1935 on one of the first exploratory expeditions to Everest, and he was the

Hillary and Tenzing's route up Everest in 1953

ADVANCING GEAR

In 1953, mountaineers carried loaded packs that weighed more than 40 pounds (18 kg). Today, climbers' packs are half as heavy or less. The wood-handled ax Hillary used on Everest was heavy and long, whereas today's axes have hollow aluminum shafts and weigh less than one pound (0.5 kg). The walkie-talkies used to communicate between camps in 1953 weighed five pounds (2.3 kg) each.[6] Today, climbers can use small, lightweight cell phones from almost anywhere on the mountain to call anywhere in the world.

During the 1953 Everest expedition, Hillary wore an outer layer consisting of a thin, windproof suit woven from cotton and nylon. His mid-layer was made of Scotland wool. Hillary also wore a synthetic base layer. Today, the materials used for base layers have greater wicking capabilities and allow for quicker evaporation. Modern outer layers are made of high-tech wind-stopping fabric, insulated with goose down, and designed for movement. Boots today have also advanced and are more weatherproof, insulated, breathable, and lightweight.

headman of the Sherpas with the Swiss team attempt on Everest in 1952.

Hillary, originally a beekeeper, was an experienced climber by 1953, having summited Mount Cook in New Zealand and the Himalayan summit of Mukut Parbat. Hillary was also part of the Everest mission to gain information with Shipton in 1951.

The expedition started in Kathmandu, the capital of Nepal. Porters would carry the 13 short tons (11.8 metric tons) of equipment, including oxygen cylinders.[5] The group hiked 170 miles (274 km) to base camp. Early on, team leader Hunt recognized Tenzing's and Hillary's strong and quick climbing abilities. The team made its way up Everest. High on the peak on May 26, Hunt sent two of the group's men to make the first summit attempt. However, due to a malfunctioning oxygen system, they were forced to turn back within 300 feet (100 m) of their goal.

For the second attempt three days later, Hunt sent Tenzing and Hillary. They set up camp higher than anyone had before, giving them a better chance for success. They started upward by 6:30 a.m. and reached the highest point on Earth at 11:30 a.m. on May 29, 1953. Hillary reports a "sense of quiet satisfaction" and disbelief.[7] He later wrote,

> *Now Tenzing and I were there: it seemed hard to believe. . . . I could see Tenzing grinning beatifically. I reached out to shake his hand, but he would have none of it. Instead, he flung his arms around my shoulders. We hugged and thumped each other on the back until forced to stop for lack of breath.*[8]

On the summit, Tenzing posed for a photo that has become one of climbing's most legendary images. He attached flags of Nepal, Britain, India, and the United

Nations to his ice ax and held it up. Tenzing and Hillary then laid offerings at the mountain's summit, including the flags from Tenzing's ax.

The next year, in 1954, an Italian team succeeded in climbing the world's second-highest peak, K2 in the Karakoram Range, at 28,251 feet (8,611 m) high.[9] The British summited the world's third-highest peak, the 28,169-foot (8,586-m) Kanchenjunga in the eastern Himalayas, in 1955.[10] Over the next decade, teams from across the world succeeded in summiting all 14 of the world's peaks higher than 26,247 feet (8,000 m). A Chinese team climbed the last, Shishapangma, which is 26,398 feet (8,046 m) high, in 1964.[11]

Tenzing placing flags on Everest's summit

Although many climbers argue against heavy use of equipment, advancing safety equipment and techniques have allowed interested people of all ages and backgrounds to explore mountain climbing.

CHAPTER 9

THE NEWEST GENERATION

In the last half of the 1900s, technology made climbing safer and improving incomes opened the door to mountaineering for a broader social base. People could travel farther and set their aspirations higher. At the same time, a new breed of mountain explorers emerged. Alpine-style climbing became more popular. Environmental concerns, in part, dictated the course climbers took.

THE NEW FACE OF EXPEDITIONS

Many early expeditions to the Himalayas were enormous endeavors. They generally involved the latest in equipment and a battalion of support, as was true of the British Everest expedition in 1953. Climbers relied on Sherpas and porters, fixed ropes, and oxygen. Yet right at the time expeditions were growing in size and cost, other climbers emerged who were approaching expeditions differently. Some climbers became known for their small, lightweight approaches, similar to Tilman and Shipton's. As Tilman once said, "Any worthwhile expedition can be planned on the back of an envelope."[1] When Hermann Buhl succeeded in climbing Nanga Parbat solo in 1953 without oxygen, he was on the cutting edge of a new approach to mountaineering, which continued growing in later years.

Artificial climbing also became standard practice in the later part of the century, again inciting debate. Instead of relying on the mountain itself to provide natural rock spires to drape a rope over or natural chock stones, artificial means were used increasingly. This growing use of artificial climbing aids such as nuts, bolts, and pitons was hotly debated. As Mallory argued,

> *The climber does best to rely on his natural abilities, which warn him whether he is overstepping the bounds of his strength. With artificial aids, he exposes himself to the possibility of sudden collapse if the apparatus fails.*[2]

Mallory's belief that nothing should come between a climber and the mountain is an ethic many climbers still adhere to.

More climbers adopted the alpine style of climbing in the 1950s, which Mummery had advocated a century earlier. One of the leading contemporary climbers to push for this style was Reinhold Messner of Italy.

SUMMITING WITHOUT SIGHT

In 2001, Eric Weihenmayer became the first climber to summit Everest without sight. Weihenmayer was born with an eye disease that made him completely blind by age 13. He was determined not to let blindness get in his way of living a full life. Weihenmayer wrestled competitively in school, then turned to mountaineering. While climbing Everest, Weihenmayer contributed his share to the climbing team. "I wanted them to put their lives in my hands as I would put mine in theirs," he said.[3] After Everest, Weihenmayer went on to climb each of the Seven Summits. He has also worked closely with Braille Without Borders, which works in developing countries to empower the visually impaired. Weihenmayer has climbed with visually impaired students in Tibet and trekked across the Andes with a team of visually impaired youth.

Reinhold Messner in 1980,
discussing his solo ascent of
Everest without an artificial
oxygen supply

In 1971, he wrote an essay titled "Murder of the Impossible," in which he argued that mountain climbing for many people was no longer a matter of skill and fortitude, but one reliant on the latest equipment. For Messner, the challenge was less about which mountains he climbed and more about how he climbed them. He exemplified the fast and light ethic, reaching numerous summits in record time on a single, lightweight push. He is best known for the first ascent of Everest without oxygen with guide Peter Habeler on May 8, 1978, putting an end to a long debate over whether it could be done.

ENVIRONMENTAL ISSUES

Messner's pioneering, lightweight style also resonated in the climbing community for environmental reasons. The large-scale sieges of the world's highest mountains and the increased climbing traffic began having an environmental impact, as climbers often left behind their trash.

In the decades following the first ascent of Everest, the mountain and its surrounding peaks became littered with oxygen bottles, tents, and garbage. In 2008, a cleanup effort was launched. Spearheaded by a Sherpa named Apa Sherpa, the effort aimed to bring down more than 11,000 pounds (4,990 kg) of trash over several years.[4] Nepal now requires that climbers pack out all trash and waste.

The use of artificial aids also became a greater environmental issue. Canadian Yvon Chouinard was a leader in advocating for clean climbing aids in the 1970s. In the big-wall climbing era in Yosemite, Chouinard climbed with many great climbers and used hard-steel pitons he made and sold. But he soon recognized the damage the iron pitons were doing to the rocks. He stopped selling the pitons and turned his attention to a "Climb Clean" campaign, along with fellow climber Robbins. He also designed and manufactured innovative aluminum alloy nuts shaped like a wedge, which largely replaced hammering pitons. Chouinard's inventions, his leadership in lightweight alpinism in North America,

Members of the Sagarmatha Pollution Control Committee clean up garbage atop peaks in Sagarmatha National Park, where Everest is located.

and his environmental advocacy influenced the newest generation of world climbers.

MODERN CLIMBERS

Climbers continue seeking new challenges across the world. One such challenge was to climb each of the Seven Summits.

In 1985, climber Dick Bass became the first to complete them all. Other climbers set their sights on ascending all 14 of the world's summits 26,247 feet (8,000 m) or higher. Messner was the first to accomplish this feat in 1986.

Some climbers, reacting at least in part to environmental concerns, turned to free climbing for new challenges. A free climb is an ascent using only one's hands and feet, strength, and skill. Climbers use gear merely for protection, in order to attach a rope

THE SEVENTH SUMMIT DEBATE

As climbers raced to be the first to ascend each of the Seven Summits, Dick Bass and Pat Morrow both lay claims to being the first. Bass completed each of the seven, completing Kosciuszko in Australia at 7,310 feet (2,228 m) high last. Morrow also climbed all seven, but he defined the seventh summit as Carstensz Pyramid in New Guinea, which rises to 16,023 feet (4,884 m).[5] Morrow claimed the peak sits on the Australian continental shelf, making it a part of the continent. A deeper look at the geologic plates beneath the island showed Carstensz Pyramid does not sit on the same tectonic plate as Australia, however, which would make it a part of Asia's tectonic plates.

The debate over which is the true seventh summit continues today. To solve the problem, some climbers resolve to climb all eight as a part of the feat to climb the continent's highest peaks.

Modern mountain climbers
often free-climb, using ropes
as a safety backup only.

CLIMBING AS A CAREER

The first people to make a living mountain climbing were guides, which was a well-paying profession for many working-class men. Sherpas have also earned a substantial living assisting foreign climbers. Then, by the mid-1900s, climbing itself became a profession. American mountaineer Lynn Hill turned her passion for climbing into a remarkable career. Throughout the 1980s and 1990s, Hill participated in climbing competitions, winning more than 30 international titles.

Other climbers make a living giving lectures, working on film projects, and writing about their experiences. Reinhold Messner is one example. He has written books, lectured, and made films about his excursions.

Countless companies also give the world's best climbers clothing and equipment in order to increase exposure of their brand names. Additionally, most expeditions today are funded by large organizations. Finally, some climbers are able to profit from climbing through corporate sponsorships.

or protect against a fall, relying on their bodies and personal strength rather than the ropes. American climber Lynn Hill perhaps best represents this emergent breed of climbers. El Capitan in Yosemite was first climbed in 1958. But Hill was the first person to free-climb it via the Nose over four days in 1993. She strove to re-climb it faster and returned to free-climb the Nose in 1994. Hill completed the climb in less than 23 hours, which was a first. Hill's epic rock-climbing career included countless new routes up hard climbs, bold first ascents, and several titles in international climbing competitions.

Other mountaineers pushed the limits through alpine-style climbing on the world's tallest peaks. In April 1991, Slovenians Andrej Stremfelj and Marko Prezel succeeded in climbing alpine style up the southwest ridge of Kangchenjunga in the Himalayas to its southern summit. Then, in 2002, German Alex Huber succeeded in climbing a difficult, technical route on the Cima Grande in Italy with only a chalk bag and special shoes for rock climbing.

New arenas were also explored. On Baffin Island, in the Canadian Arctic, vertical walls rise out of the fjords. In 1996, three Americans took more than five weeks to climb Polar Sun Spire, one of the largest, most difficult walls at 4,429 feet (1,350 m) high.[6] In 1998, Alex Lowe and five others conquered the 3,773-foot (1,150 m) vertical face of Great Sail Peak on Baffin Island.[7] Other climbers found new big walls to climb in Madagascar and Pakistan. Patagonia also offered new mountaineering challenges. One goal for alpinists there was the traverse of the Torre Group of four mountains, which are great peaks in an inhospitable, windy region of the world. Several climbers had made attempts in previous

decades. But not until 2008 was the traverse completed by Rolando Gariobotti and Colin Haley between January 21 and January 24.

Today there are still hundreds of unclimbed peaks throughout the world, begging to be explored. And given the nature of mountaineers, they will continue exploring and pushing the limits of what is humanly possible. As Muir once said, "The mountains are calling and I must go."[8]

New discoveries on conquered frontiers and first summits of new peaks continue inspiring mountain climbers today.

TIMELINE

1492 Antoine de Ville summits Mont Aiguille in France on the orders of King Charles VIII.

1786 Michel-Gabriel Paccard and Jacques Balmat summit Mont Blanc in the Alps on August 8, marking the beginning of mountaineering as a sport.

1854–1865 The golden age of mountaineering takes place.

1857 The Alpine Club is established in London, England, on December 22.

1865 On July 14, Edward Whymper summits the Matterhorn with six others. Four fall to their death during the descent.

1865 Adolphus Moore, guide Melchior Anderegg, and their party ascend the Brenva Face of Mont Blanc on July 14–15.

1879 Albert Mummery and his guide, Alexander Burgener, ascend the Matterhorn via Zmutt Ridge on September 3.

1892 Martin Conway launches the first exploratory expedition to the Karakoram Range.

1895 In August, Mummery attempts to climb Nanga Parbat and disappears.

1897 Guide Matthias Zurbriggen summits Aconcagua on January 14.

1902 The American Alpine Club is founded.

1924 George Mallory and Andrew "Sandy" Irvine climb near the summit of Everest in June but are never seen again.

1936 Bill Tilman and Noel Odell reach the summit of Nanda Devi without supplemental oxygen.

1950 A French team summits the 26,545-foot (8,091-m) peak Annapurna on June 3.

1953 On May 29, Tenzing Norgay and Edmund Hillary become the first to summit Everest.

1957 Royal Robbins and two others make the technical rock ascent of Half Dome in Yosemite.

1958 Warren Harding and several others ascend the vertical route called The Nose of El Capitan in Yosemite for the first time.

1978 Reinhold Messner and Peter Habeler reach the summit of Everest without oxygen on May 8.

1985 Dick Bass is the first person to ascend each of the Seven Summits.

1986 Messner becomes the first person to complete an ascent of all 14 of the world's 26,247-foot (8,000 m) peaks.

ESSENTIAL FACTS ABOUT MOUNTAIN EXPLORATION

KEY DISCOVERIES AND THEIR IMPACTS

On August 8, 1786, Michel-Gabriel Paccard and Jacques Balmat summited Mont Blanc in the Alps, opening the door to further mountain exploration. In 1934, Bill Tilman reached the summit of Nanda Devi without supplemental oxygen, setting the stage for future alpine-style expeditions.

In the 1840s, the ice ax made climbing easier and safer. Advancements to crampons, pitons, nuts, bolts, ice screws, and camming devices through the next century made vertical rock and ice ascents possible. Oxygen gear allowed mountain explorers to venture higher, culminating in the ascent of Everest.

KEY PLAYERS

Albert Mummery is known as the father of modern alpinism.

Bill Tilman and Eric Shipton were renowned alpine-style explorers in the Himalayas.

Tenzing Norgay and Edmund Hillary were the first to ascend Everest.

Reinhold Messner made the first ascent of Everest without oxygen.

Lynn Hill is a prominent free climber of the second half of the 1900s.

KEY TECHNOLOGY

Ice ax, crampons, pitons, nuts, bolts, nylon rope, oxygen gear

QUOTE

"The true mountaineer is a wanderer . . . a man who loves to be where no human being has been before, who delights in gripping rocks that have previously never felt the touch of human fingers . . . Equally, whether he succeeds or fails, he delights in the fun and jollity of the struggle."

–Albert Mummery

GLOSSARY

acclimatization

The process of adapting to increasingly higher altitudes.

altitude sickness

The effects of high altitude on the body as a result of lower air pressure and thus reduced oxygen in the body; symptoms include shortness of breath, headaches, and nausea.

backcountry

An unpopulated, remote wilderness area.

bivouac

A temporary overnight camp set up on the mountainside with little gear.

bolt

An artificial climbing device hammered or drilled into a rock to assist an ascent or protect against a fall.

carabiner

A metal ring that has a spring-loaded side that can be opened and clipped to ropes.

chock stone

A rock jammed in a crevice.

crevasse

A deep crack in a glacier.

ice screw

A steel rod with a ring on one end screwed into ice to act as an anchor for climbers.

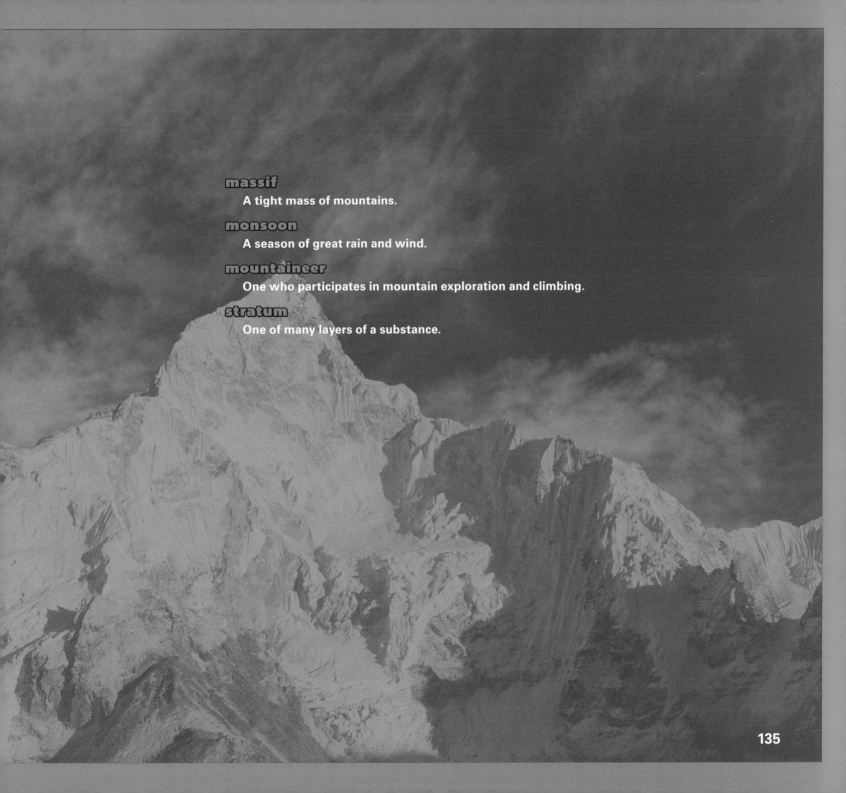

massif
A tight mass of mountains.

monsoon
A season of great rain and wind.

mountaineer
One who participates in mountain exploration and climbing.

stratum
One of many layers of a substance.

135

ADDITIONAL RESOURCES

SELECTED BIBLIOGRAPHY

Bonington, Chris. *The Climbers: A History of Mountaineering*. London: BBC, 1992. Print.

Douglas, Ed, et al. *Mountaineers: Great Tales of Bravery and Conquest*. New York: Smithsonian/DK, 2011. Print.

Lewis-Jones, Huw. *Mountain Heroes: Portraits of Adventure*. Guilford, CT: FalconGuides, 2012. Print.

Venables, Stephen. *First Ascent*. Buffalo, NY: Firefly, 2008. Print.

FURTHER READINGS

Currie, Stephen. *The Himalayas*. Detroit, MI: Lucent/Thomson Gale, 2005. Print.

Salkeld, Audrey. *Climbing Everest: Tales of Triumph and Tragedy on the World's Highest Mountain*. Washington DC: National Geographic, 2003. Print.

WEB SITES

To learn more about exploring mountains, visit ABDO Publishing Company online at **www.abdopublishing.com**. Web sites about exploring mountains are featured on our Book Links page. These links are routinely monitored and updated to provide the most current information available.

FOR MORE INFORMATION

For more information on this subject, contact or visit the following organizations:

American Alpine Club/Mountaineering Museum

710 Tenth Street, Suite 100
Golden, CO 80401
303-384-0110
http://www.americanalpineclub.org
The American Alpine Club (AAC) and Mountaineering Museum provide information on mountain conservation and support and inspiration for climbers. The AAC also helps sponsor the Bradford Washburn American Mountaineering Museum and has an extensive mountaineering library.

Appalachian Mountain Club

5 Joy Street
Boston, MA 02108
617-523-0636
http://www.outdoors.org
Since 1876, the Appalachian Mountain Club has supported mountain conservation, study, education, and recreation. The club hosts activities in various areas and offers programs for family and youth interested in mountains. They also maintain huts and lodges across the Appalachian Mountains.

SOURCE NOTES

CHAPTER 1. MOUNTAIN EXPLORATION

1. "Mount Everest." *Encyclopædia Britannica*. Encyclopædia Britannica, 2013. Web. 29 July 2013.

2. Stephen Venables. *Voices from the Mountains: 40 True-Life Stories of Unforgettable Adventure, Drama, and Human Endurance*. Pleasantville, NY: Reader's Digest, 2006. Print. 135.

3. Ibid.

4. Jack D. Ives, consultant ed. *Mountains: The Illustrated Library of the Earth*. Emmaus, PA: Rodale, 1994. Print. 22, 47.

5. "Mount Elbrus." *Encyclopædia Britannica*. Encyclopædia Britannica, 2013. Web. 29 July 2013.

6. "Kilimanjaro." *Encyclopædia Britannica*. Encyclopædia Britannica, 2013. Web. 29 July 2013.

7. "Mount Kosciuszko." *Encyclopædia Britannica*. Encyclopædia Britannica, 2013. Web. 29 July 2013.

8. "Vinson Massif." *Encyclopædia Britannica*. Encyclopædia Britannica, 2013. Web. 29 July 2013.

9. "Andes Mountains." *Encyclopædia Britannica*. Encyclopædia Britannica, 2013. Web. 29 July 2013.

10. Mike Hamill. *Climbing the Seven Summits: A Comprehensive Guide to the Continents' Highest Peaks*. Seattle, WA: Mountaineers, 2012. Print. 56.

11. Ibid.

12. Chris Bonington. *The Climbers: A History of Mountaineering*. London: BBC Books, 1992. Print. 58.

13. Mike Hamill. *Climbing the Seven Summits: A Comprehensive Guide to the Continents' Highest Peaks*. Seattle, WA: Mountaineers, 2012. Print. 197–199.

CHAPTER 2. EARLY CLIMBERS

1. Chris Bonington and Audrey Salkeld, eds. *Heroic Climbs: A Celebration of World Mountaineering*. Seattle, WA: Mountaineers, 1994. Print. 12.

2. Ed Douglas, et al. *Mountaineers: Great Tales of Bravery and Conquest*. New York: Smithsonian/DK, 2011. Print. 25.

3. Ibid. 22.

4. Stephen Venables. *First Ascent*. Buffalo, NY: Firefly, 2008. Print. 12.

5. Ed Douglas, et al. *Mountaineers: Great Tales of Bravery and Conquest*. New York: Smithsonian/DK, 2011. Print. 30.

6. Ibid. 74.

7. Stephen Venables. *First Ascent*. Buffalo, NY: Firefly, 2008. Print. 11.

8. Ed Douglas, et al. *Mountaineers: Great Tales of Bravery and Conquest*. New York: Smithsonian/DK, 2011. Print. 20–21.

9. Ibid. 36–37.

10. Ibid. 38.

CHAPTER 3. SUMMITS, SCIENCE, SURVEYING, AND SIGHTSEEING

1. Ed Douglas, et al. *Mountaineers: Great Tales of Bravery and Conquest*. New York: Smithsonian/DK, 2011. Print. 56.

2. Ibid. 60.

3. Stephen Venables. *First Ascent*. Buffalo, NY: Firefly, 2008. Print. 17.

4. Chris Bonington. *The Climbers: A History of Mountaineering*. London: BBC Books, 1992. Print. 25.

5. Stephen E. Ambrose. *Lewis & Clark: Voyage of Discovery*. 1st ed. Washington DC: National Geographic, 1998. Print. 151.

6. Roger Lawrence Williams. "A Region of Astonishing Beauty:" *The Botanical Exploration of the Rocky Mountains*. Lanham, MD: R. Rinehart, 2003. *Google Book Search*. Web. 23 Aug. 2013.

7. Ed Douglas, et al. *Mountaineers: Great Tales of Bravery and Conquest*. New York: Smithsonian/DK, 2011. Print. 102.

8. Ibid.

9. Ibid. 76.

CHAPTER 4. THE GOLDEN AGE OF MOUNTAINEERING

1. Ed Douglas, et al. *Mountaineers: Great Tales of Bravery and Conquest*. New York: Smithsonian/DK, 2011. Print. 115.

2. Ibid.

3. Chris Bonington. *The Climbers: A History of Mountaineering*. London: BBC Books, 1992. Print. 34.

4. Stephen Venables. *First Ascent*. Buffalo, NY: Firefly, 2008. Print. 32.

5. "Sierra Club History." *Sierra Club*. Sierra Club, 2013. Web. 23 Aug. 2013.

6. Ed Douglas, et al. *Mountaineers: Great Tales of Bravery and Conquest*. New York: Smithsonian/DK, 2011. Print. 140.

CHAPTER 5. NEW FRONTIERS

1. "What Is a Colorado 14er?" *Colorado*. Colorado Tourism Office, 2013. Web. 23 Aug. 2013.

2. Lisa Foster. *Rocky Mountain National Park: The Complete Hiking Guide*. Englewood, CO: Westcliffe, 2005. *Google Book Search*. Web. 23 Aug. 2013.

3. "Who Was John Muir?" *Sierra Club*. Sierra Club, 2013. Web. 23 Aug. 2013.

4. Ed Douglas, et al. *Mountaineers: Great Tales of Bravery and Conquest*. New York: Smithsonian/DK, 2011. Print. 170.

5. Chris Bonington. *The Climbers: A History of Mountaineering*. London: BBC Books, 1992. Print. 56.

6. Huw Lewis-Jones. *Mountain Heroes: Portraits of Adventure*. Guilford, CT: FalconGuides, 2012. Print. 149.

7. Ed Douglas, et al. *Mountaineers: Great Tales of Bravery and Conquest*. New York: Smithsonian/DK, 2011. Print. 176.

SOURCE NOTES CONTINUED

8. Huw Lewis-Jones. *Mountain Heroes: Portraits of Adventure*. Guilford, CT: FalconGuides, 2012. Print. 148.

9. Mike Hamill. *Climbing the Seven Summits: A Comprehensive Guide to the Continents' Highest Peaks*. Seattle, WA: Mountaineers, 2012. Print. 51–53.

10. "Altitude Physiology, Sleep and Exercise." *Institute for Altitude Medicine at Telluride*. Institute For Altitude Medicine, 2013. Web. 23 Aug. 2013.

11. "Chimborazo." *Encyclopædia Britannica*. Encyclopædia Britannica, 2013. Web. 29 July 2013.

12. "Altitude Physiology, Sleep and Exercise." *Institute for Altitude Medicine at Telluride*. Institute For Altitude Medicine, 2013. Web. 23 Aug. 2013.

13. Frederic V. Hartemann and Robert Hauptman. *The Mountain Encyclopedia*. Lanham, MD: Scarecrow, 2005. Print. 155.

14. "Avalanches." *National Geographic*. National Geographic Society, 2013. Web. 25 Aug. 2013.

CHAPTER 6. NEW PEAKS

1. "Mount Aconcagua." *Encyclopædia Britannica*. Encyclopædia Britannica, 2013. Web. 25 Aug. 2013.

2. "Mount Robson Provincial Park." *British Columbia: BC Parks*. British Columbia: Ministry of Environment, n.d. Web. 25 Aug. 2013.

3. "Mount McKinley." *Encyclopædia Britannica*. Encyclopædia Britannica, 2013. Web. 25 Aug. 2013.

4. Ibid.

5. Mike Hamill. *Climbing the Seven Summits: A Comprehensive Guide to the Continents' Highest Peaks*. Seattle, WA: Mountaineers, 2012. Print. 135.

6. "Mount Huascarán." *Encyclopædia Britannica*. Encyclopædia Britannica, 2013. Web. 6 Sept. 2013.

CHAPTER 7. GREATER CHALLENGES

1. Audrey Salkeld, ed. and foreword by Chris Bonington. *World Mountaineering: The World's Greatest Mountains by the World's Greatest Mountaineers*. Boston: Bulfinch, 1998. Print. 50.

2. Ibid. 54–56.

3. Mike Hamill. *Climbing the Seven Summits: A Comprehensive Guide to the Continents' Highest Peaks*. Seattle, WA: Mountaineers, 2012. Print. 29.

4. Chris Bonington. *The Climbers: A History of Mountaineering*. London: BBC Books, 1992. Print. 81.

5. Matt Perkins. "Rock Climbing Ethics: A Historical Perspective." *Northwest Mountaineering Journal*. Northwest Mountaineering Journal, 2005. Web. 25 Aug. 2013.

6. Brian Clark Howard. "Yosemite's Iconic El Capitan Mapped in High-Res 3-D." *National Geographic*. National Geographic Society, 12 June 2013. Web. 25 Aug. 2013.

7. Matt Perkins. "Rock Climbing Ethics: A Historical Perspective." *Northwest Mountaineering Journal*. Northwest Mountaineering Journal, 2005. Web. 25 Aug. 2013.

CHAPTER 8. TOP OF THE WORLD

1. Reinhold Messner. *Annapurna: 50 Years of Expeditions into the Death Zone*. 1st ed. Seattle, WA: Mountaineers, 2000. Print. 11.

2. Frederic V. Hartemann and Robert Hauptman. *The Mountain Encyclopedia*. Lanham, MD: Scarecrow, 2005. Print. 155.

3. "Dhaulagiri I." *Encyclopædia Britannica*. Encyclopædia Britannica, 2013. Web. 25 Aug. 2013.

4. "Annapurna." *Encyclopædia Britannica*. Encyclopædia Britannica, 2013. Web. 25 Aug. 2013.

5. Stephen Venables. *First Ascent*. Buffalo, NY: Firefly, 2008. Print. 79–80.

6. "Everest Climbing Gear: Hillary to Hilaree." *National Geographic*. National Geographic Society, 2013. Web. 25 Aug. 2013.

7. Chris Bonington and Audrey Salkeld, eds. *Heroic Climbs: A Celebration of World Mountaineering*. Seattle, WA: Mountaineers, 1994. Print. 162.

8. Ibid.

9. Ed Douglas, et al. *Mountaineers: Great Tales of Bravery and Conquest*. New York: Smithsonian/DK, 2011. Print. 271.

10. Ibid. 273.

11. Stephen Venables. *First Ascent*. Buffalo, NY: Firefly, 2008. Print. 85.

CHAPTER 9. THE NEWEST GENERATION

1. Mark Harvey. *The National Outdoor Leadership School's Wilderness Guide: The Classic Handbook, Revised and Updated*. New York: Simon, 1999. Print. 32.

2. "First Without Oxygen." *NOVA Online Adventure*. PBS/NOVA Online, 2000. Web. 25 Aug. 2013.

3. Huw Lewis-Jones. *Mountain Heroes: Portraits of Adventure*. Guilford, CT: FalconGuides, 2012. Print. 241.

4. Lukas I. Alpert. "Mount Everest Expedition Climbs up World's Largest Peak to Clear 5 1/2 Tons of Garbage Off Mountain." *Daily News*. NYDailyNews.com, 6 April 2011. Web. 25 Aug. 2013.

5. Mike Hamill. *Climbing the Seven Summits: A Comprehensive Guide to the Continents' Highest Peaks*. Seattle, WA: Mountaineers, 2012. Print. 17.

6. Lindsay Griffin. "New Route on Polar Sun Spire." *BMC*. British Mountaineering Council, 6 Aug. 2012. Web. 25 Aug. 2013.

7. Stephen Venables. *First Ascent*. Buffalo, NY: Firefly, 2008. Print. 164–166.

8. William Frederic Badè. "The Life and Letters of John Muir." *Sierra Club*. Sierra Club, 2013. Web. 25 Aug. 2013.

INDEX

ABOUT THE AUTHOR

Laura Perdew is an author, middle school teacher, and novice mountaineer. She writes fiction and nonfiction for children of all ages and has also published *Kids on the Move! Colorado*, a guide for parents traveling through Colorado with small children. Perdew lives in Boulder, right in the foothills of the Colorado Rockies, with her husband and twin boys.

ABOUT THE CONSULTANT

Maurice Isserman has a bachelor of arts in history from Reed College and a PhD in American history from the University of Rochester. Isserman has received many academic honors throughout his career, including a Mellon fellowship at Harvard University and the Fulbright Distinguished Chair at Russia's Moscow State University. His 2008 book, *Fallen Giants: A History of Himalayan Mountaineering from the Age of Empire to the Age of Extremes,* coauthored with Stewart Weaver, won that year's Banff Mountain Festival book prize as well as the National Outdoor Book Award for best mountaineering history.